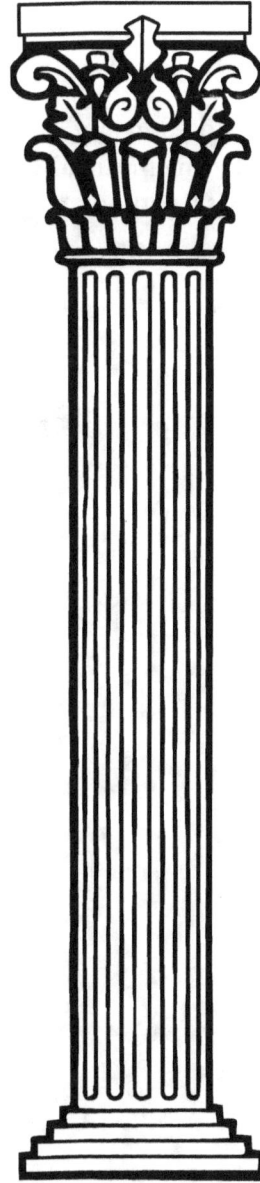

WHERE THERE'S A WILL THERE'S A WRONG WAY

SUSAN SPARROW

Copyright © 2019 Susan Sparrow

All rights reserved.
No part of this publication may be reproduced, stored in any retrieval system, or transmitted in any form or by any means, mechanical, photocopying, recording, or otherwise, without permission in writing from the publisher.

Book written and illustrated by Susan Sparrow.

Book layout by Cerutti Graphic Design

Manufactured in the United States of America.

For more information, please contact:
Publishing Concepts LLC
6590 Scanlan Avenue
St. Louis MO 63139
www.PublishingConceptsLLC.com

ISBN 13: 978-1-933635-35-4

LCCN:
FAMILY & LAW
1 2 3 4 5 6 7 8 9 10

This is a true story

*To Mom and Dad
For your love, generosity,
validation, and respect.*

"A ship in the harbor is safe,
but that's not what ships are for..."

BENJAMIN FRANKLIN

OPENING THOUGHTS

For most of us, the thought of losing a parent is the worst thing that could ever happen. As we grow older, that fear does not diminish. We cannot imagine a world without our beloved Moms and Dads. When the inevitable happens, and we are suddenly forced into facing their death, we are obligated to deal with complex issues we never imagined.

Everyone mourns differently. Some of us grieve more demonstratively while others hold their pain deep inside. Even the range of emotions within the same family can be polar opposites.

How is this possible? It's simple, people don't share the same capacity for love. Love comes in many forms and depths. That is why relationships are so different, even within close families.

I was born with an artistic, romantic nature. My capacity to love has always been deep—to the marrow of my bones. That is how I am wired. In contrast, I had family members who rarely showed emotion. Unfortunately, the only time they opened up was after a few drinks.

Facing the death of a parent can bring out the best in people. It can also bring out the worst.

My purpose in writing this book is to share the worst-case scenario of what happened to me following the death of my mother. The death of not only the woman I cherished most, but also the death of her family, as well as my parent's legacy.

FACING THE INEVITABLE

None of us want to face the inevitable—death. We don't want to think about it. We don't want to talk about it. We don't want to do anything about it. So we don't.

It's too scary to think about, but you know what? It's selfish not to ponder.

Having an up-to-date, legal will is the most unselfish thing you can do for your family.

Passing the buck, expecting your family to deal with death issues—only you can handle—is a breach of responsibility. It can cause havoc and heartbreak that can never heal.

Most of us never think in terms of having an "estate". So, simply think in terms of all your "stuff". If you have a home, car, computer, or collection of anything from antique dolls, to old tools your grandfather left you—you have an estate. Most of us worked very hard, all our lives, to provide for our families. Most of the folks I talk to agree we all have too much stuff.

Thinking that our spouse (or children) will best decide what to do with our "stuff", doesn't begin to address the issue.

Maybe we made a will in our 30s as a new spouse or parent. But what if that was wife (or husband) number one, and we're now on spouse number three and child and step-child number five? Clearly, the complex history of blended families is bound to cause issues.

So, thinking an out-of-date will will cover your needs today is a huge mistake.

Most of us have emotional and financial attachments to our "stuff". It would break our hearts to see our ex-daughter-in-law wearing jewelry meant for our own daughter.

Once items are "removed" from your home, they will most likely never be returned.

Sentimental attachments mean a lot to us.

Estate fights often involve family possessions with very little monetary value outside our families. I knew a family who fought over a salt and pepper shaker set their mother had in her kitchen for a lifetime.

It's not always about the money; in most cases, conflict emerges from these strong emotional ties to the object.

Making a will takes courage. You may make decisions that upset members of your family. Too bad! Remember, this is YOUR will to distribute YOUR stuff.

No one is entitled to your stuff. No one. Creating a will, and updating it, is your unselfish gift to those with whom you choose to share your possessions and your legacy.

Do not let GUILT guide your decision making.

HOW TO START

Start with a list, or a series of lists. Begin listing your major assets, homes, cars, properties, etc. Then list the people close to you, with whom you wish to include in your will. Besides family, this could include institutions such as the American Cancer Society, churches, schools, or your local no-kill animal shelter.

Assets, money, and beneficiaries WILL change over time, that is why it's wise to look at your current will at least once every year. People pass away unexpectedly, others simply drift from our lives.

Do you really want to leave your Model-T Ford to your cousin who was incarcerated since you last updated your will?

Write down your questions and concerns, and give it thought and time. When you think you have enough rough work drawn up, call an attorney, and get the ball rolling.

I promise you, once you take the time, spend the money, and have a will (or trust) legally drawn up, you will feel better falling asleep at night. Getting it handled NOW, while you are able to make wise decisions, is one of the smartest moves you will ever make.

It's not easy, but nothing worthwhile ever is.

REASONS WHY PEOPLE PROCRASTINATE ABOUT WRITING A WILL

- Laziness. "It takes too much time, work and money."
- Fear of death. "If I don't face it, it won't happen."
- It's not my problem. "I'll be dead; let them fight over it."
- Passing the buck. "They'll work it out somehow."
- Fear of upsetting others. "What if they get mad at me?"
- Fear of responsibility. "It's too big a job for me to handle. I don't have the money."
- Belief that the estate isn't big enough. "We're not the Vanderbilts."
- Belief that your spouse will handle it. Do they know your private intentions?
- Belief that lawyers and advisors will handle it. They can handle the legal proceedings, only YOU can handle the personal decisions.
- "I made a will years ago. That's good enough (even if it was three wives ago)."

People need to know that an out-of-date will (or trust) is a potential disaster waiting to happen. It could destroy the lives of those you love most!

CONTENTS

Introduction	xix
Common Myths about Wills	xxi

PART ONE
HOW IT ALL BEGAN
MY FAMILY

1	Dad	3
2	Mom	5
3	Brother #1	8
4	Brother #2	9
5	Brother #3	11
6	The Final Straw	14
7	Brother #4	16
8	My Sister	18
9	My Baby, Brother #5	20
10	Susan	23

PART TWO
THE NIGHTMARE BEGINS

11	Coming Apart at the Seams	31
12	Losing Dad	32
13	The Black Books	38
14	Wrestling for the Wheel of the Titanic	40
15	The In-Laws	42
16	Dad's Dying Wish	45

17	The Corruption Escalates	47
18	Hitting Close to Home	49
19	Mom's Farm Up North	51
20	"The Prodigal"—Skulking in the Shadows	53
21	Rocking the Boat	56
22	Mom's Death	58
23	The Nightmare Begins	64
24	Reaching Out for Help	65
25	The First Meeting	67
26	Six Months after Mom's Death	69
27	Revisiting Mom's Mansion	70
28	"Merry Christmas, Susan"	72
29	The Ultimate Insult	73
30	Justice for All?	75
31	Preparing for Trial by Deposition	77
32	Building My Case	79
33	Attorneys Lying under Oath	82
34	The Open House	84
35	My Rolex Watch	86
36	The IRS	87
37	Six Against One	89
38	Going the Distance	94
39	The Final Insult	96

PART THREE
LESSONS LEARNED

40	The Aftermath	103
41	If Your Legacy Matters to You	105
42	Money	106
43	Recipe for Health Estate Plan	108
44	Choosing an Executor	109
45	Choosing an Executor with Character	112
46	Beware of Gender Discrimination	115

47	Failing the Bar	116
48	The Tricks Evil Lawyers Play	118
49	Choosing the Right Attorney	121
50	Facing the Inevitable	122
51	Keeping Grounded	124
52	Susan's Truisms	126
53	For the Record	128
54	Update: How Can They Do That?	129
55	Mourning on Many Levels: How I Survived	131
56	"For Whom the Bell Tolls"	135
57	"Aggravation Follows Me"	137
58	The Greatest Gift of All	139

*****

Acknowledgments 140
Bibliography 141
Anyway 142

INTRODUCTION

Research shows that up to seventy percent of estate transitions (wills) fail. Even if that percentage were cut in half, it remains a serious breakdown in the final distribution of ones' assets. Regardless of the value of the estate, the location in the world, or legal procedures involved, most wills fail. No matter how loving parents may be toward their children, no matter how diligent they are in preparing a will, over two-thirds of all the estate transitions will not accomplish what the parents had hoped regarding the intended distribution of their assets. As a direct result, most families will be scarred by the trauma and many families self-destruct.

While there are dozens of books on the market about how to prepare and execute a will, there is no information available, that I am aware of, about why so many wills fail? What is missing? What elements contribute to the event that I call, "the estate nightmare?" How can we prevent these negative outcomes from happening in our family? And, perhaps most important, how do we heal from the aftermath of a failed will?

This is the story of my estate nightmare, a worst-case scenario of what can happen to an heir despite the careful planning of loving, generous parents. The value of an estate is an insignificant factor when determining the amount of anguish involved when distribution turns into a family horror story. Failed wills are not only about the amount of money or other assets lost, they are about the amount of pain suffered by family members. These can be deep wounds that leave scars that never heal.

Burying my Mother and my Father whom I adored, was less painful to me than the emotional torture endured in the seven-year dissolution of their thirty million dollar estate. Knowing my business-smart Dad and my devoutly caring Mom as I did, I never would have believed the fiasco that occurred when it came to dividing their estate fairly among their seven children. I am not unique in this situation. Millions of people every day have to face estate issues. After what happened to me, I became determined to get to the root of why so many wills fail. I was desperate to find some beauty in the ashes of what remained of my family's life. My journey has been difficult. But if what I learned along the way can keep one daughter or one son from being subjected to the pure evil I suffered at the hands of my siblings, their advisors, and their attorneys, then I will have accomplished my goal.

This book is intended as a wakeup call meant to educate you, the reader, as to the potential dangers awaiting your family that may have never occurred to you in the wake of your parents' passing.

COMMON MYTHS ABOUT WILLS

That you don't have an "estate", therefore, you do NOT need a will.

That healthy people do not need wills.

That wills are only for old people with lots of money.

That your family will not fight over your estate / or your parents' estate.

That in-laws are equal to blood heirs and "entitled" to your estate.

That your family will respect your or your parents' wishes once a death occurs.

That relatives or friends can prevent an estate dispute.

That all lawyers are honest and follow the rule of law.

That lawyers don't play games with peoples' estates, favoring one heir over another for profit.

That there is such a thing as a fool-proof will.

That executors, attorneys, certified public accountants, certified financial planners, estate planners, bankers, realtors, developers or family members are morally required to be scrupulous (honest) in distributing the decedents' assets.

That the laws and courts will protect you as an heir and beneficiary.

That the distribution of family assets will be handled in a prompt, transparent, ethical, and respectful way by the executor, immediately following the death of the parent.

That "fairness" in the final distribution of your parents (estate) ALWAYS occurs.

Remember that a myth is fictitious, make-believe. It never happens.

PART ONE

How It All Began
My Family

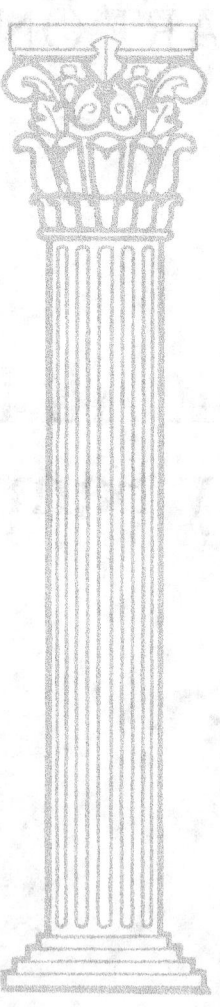

1

DAD

My Father was a self-made man who started life with few advantages and worked for over forty years to give his seven children every benefit life denied him. Having grown up with an absent alcoholic Father during the Great Depression, Dad distinguished himself as a Navy pilot during the Second World War.

Dad's career in the automobile business began on the East coast after the war. Dad started at a small dealership selling used cars. This was the early 1950s and opportunities for advancement were abundant for hard-working, smart, ambitious G.I.s.

As time progressed job advantages in the heart of the auto industry, lured my parents to relocate to the Midwest. Dad had started with a dream to work in the automobile industry and now that dream was beginning to take off. Dad was in the big leagues now, after years of climbing the corporate ladders of Ford and Chrysler. He had risen to executive vice president of both corporations as well as named to the board of directors. My Father's job was in sales and marketing designed to build bridges between the corporation and the car dealers, who were considered independents. It was his job to troubleshoot any problems that they might have and to motivate them to achieve greater numbers in sales. Dad traveled the country Monday through Friday, which was hard on both he and my Mom who had four children by now. My parents sacrificed a lot during those early years, but that was what their "Greatest Generation" did. Dad became a great motivational speaker and was well respected by his colleagues all over America.

My Father never had the financial opportunity to become an independent car dealer himself, but he always dreamed of one day helping his sons become dealers. At that time in auto history, automobile dealers made big money. As my

Dad's career reached its summit, my brothers' careers had just begun.

Becoming a car dealer not only took a lot of money, it took connections and the knowledge needed to run a franchise. When Dad believed the time and location was right, he "bought" dealerships for each of my brothers. Dad (and Mom) had invested their millions in their sons' futures. His considerable influence, contacts, and financial resources set them up. He not only gave them a leg up, he catapulted them over the wall. Dad ran the show and everyone knew it.

Along with the headaches all businesses have, come advantages few other businesses enjoy. Successful car dealers, historically, were treated to a variety of perks. If a dealer met his quota for a sales period, he could win a free trip to Europe or Hawaii. Prize points were also awarded as rewards for sales incentives, which enabled dealers or their wives to choose free gifts from catalogs. Dad was delighted and proud when my brothers did well. By the same token, the auto industry had more than its share of downturns. Over time when one son couldn't make payroll or another son was in danger of losing his franchise, Dad bailed them out. The bailouts were not in terms of hundreds of dollars. More often than not they were in the thousands, if not hundreds of thousands, even millions of dollars. Dad, always willing to help, never let one of his sons down.

My Father was a larger than life, John Wayne, type of character. Devoutly Catholic and generous in raising millions of dollars for charities. He was devoted to Mom and their marriage lasted fifty years until the day he died.

My parents started with nothing but worked, with no help from anyone, to achieve their American Dream.

They alone, built a fortune. It was THEIR money and THEIR decisions on how it was to pass on to the next generation.

Sadly, the men handling their estate, (which had passed after my Father's death to my Mother) decided otherwise.

My family was about to implode from within destroying Dad's entire legacy. I saw the iceberg coming, unfortunately – there was little I could do.

2

MOM

Born in 1920, Mom was from a generation of women who were raised to cater to the needs of men. To get a perspective on the era, consider that Abraham Lincoln's eldest son, Robert Todd Lincoln, died on July 26, 1926. Mom was six years old when the son of Abraham Lincoln died. It is hard to imagine understanding how the roles of women changed so dramatically in my Mother's near eighty-year lifespan. In Mom's world, anything men did was deemed more important than anything women did. No matter how brilliant or stupid a man might be, he was still held in higher esteem than any woman. Women were, by virtue of their birth, born second-class citizens. This was very true for Mom and it was the eyes through which she saw the world.

Mom was a tiny, fragile beauty who looked like Vivien Leigh. When Dad entered a room he had the presence of a giant sequoia. Mom though could only be compared to a wispy willow, someone who might break if you hugged her too tightly. Though Mom and Dad had begun their married life with nothing but a deep love for each other, one thing was certain: Mom was not cut out to have a large family. That was Dad's dream, not hers. In fact, Mom suffered two miscarriages, which compromised her health. Still, she complied out of love for her husband and for following both the religious and social roles of being a good wife and a good Mother, eventually having seven children. Mom was taught by her times to allow men to lead and control.

There was no money when my parents were first married. Mom reminisced about the time Dad worked at night as a bartender while going to college on the GI Bill after the war. His young bride worked as a hatcheck girl. Dad also worked as a Fuller Brush man in what little spare time he had. Mom liked to tell the story of the night they had no food in their tiny apartment, so they each looked in their coat pockets and came up with a nickel between them. Mom and Dad knew who they were and knew exactly where they came from: Shanty Irish.

After getting married at the end of the war, with nothing to their name but a dream to build a future together, a deep faith in God, and a wonderful devotion to each other, Dad always promised Mom that someday he would have her "dripping in diamonds." As they struggled to build their life together, Mom said they often laughed about that far-fetched promise. Mom didn't care. It was really Dad's promise to himself that if he could ever find a way, he would give his beautiful bride everything in life she ever wanted. As Dad rose to prominence in the auto industry he started designing and buying Mom fabulous jewelry. Of course, Mom loved his gifts. She was a girly girl who appreciated fine things including china, art, antiques, and jewelry.

As they traveled the world together Mom starred as Dad's beautiful corporate wife. Mom met presidents, movie stars, even the Pope. Dad always said Mom had the best "street smarts" of anyone he had ever known. If she suspected a cheater, she never would trust that person again. Quite often Dad would run it by Mom when he thought of promoting one guy or firing another at work. Mom had met most of the men and she had great instincts when it came to judging character. Dad always bragged that she was seldom wrong.

As Mom's first-born daughter we shared many things, including the same tastes in music and antiques. We also shared the same value system. We believed that a woman should always be a lady and look like a lady. In a time when many women no longer felt the need to dress up, when they went out with unkempt hair wearing sweatpants, my Mom refused to leave her house without her hair and make-up done. She said taking the time to look beautiful made her feel "complete" and ready to take on the world. A woman who took great pride in her appearance, Mom could never understand why "younger gals often looked like unmade beds."

Dad was always proud to have a grand lady on his arm, a woman who men flirted with until she was well into her 70s. As an executive's wife, Mom had a beautiful wardrobe meticulously kept in garment bags in several large closets throughout her home. Never once did Dad ever complain about Mom spending money on the tailored suits and silk blouses in which she looked her best. On the contrary, if she found a suit she loved at J.C. Penney's, Dad would say, "Honey, we've got money now. I'm taking you to Saks, Bonwit's, or Nordstrom." He would even go with her when she tried on clothes and if she found something special he would buy it for her in every color.

My Mother never lost her humility and her knowledge of who she and Dad were and where they came from. A throwback to being raised in the Depression, she never wasted anything. She gave generously to charities she believed in and she gave every person she met the benefit of the doubt. The one thing Mom hated was arrogance of any kind.

Mom had an adorable personality that made her a very memorable person.

She was overwhelmingly sweet one minute and witty and sassy the next. Until the day he died, Dad used to say "Isn't she cute?" Long into their fiftieth year of marriage, I would see Dad pinch Mom on the tushy as he passed her in the kitchen. To me, that said it all.

My Mom suffered from the "disease to please." She lived most of her life with the inability to form her lips around the word "no." For that reason, people took advantage of her, especially her own children.

3

BROTHER #1

I cannot remember a time when my older brother liked me. I can still recall the day he took my new black kitten by the tail, swung it over his head, and hurled it into a wall, leaving me hysterical. I was three: he was five. From early on I learned to avoid him for my very survival.

My Dad gave him the nickname, "halfway." I never knew what that meant, but the way Dad said it, I knew it couldn't be good. As I grew older and discovered what it meant, I decided to be the opposite. I never did anything "halfway." Maybe that is why we grew up as opposites.

After college, my brother followed my Father into the automobile business. As our generation of men were being drafted into the war in Vietnam my brother decided to go to law school to avoid any military duty. Even though the war was hugely unpopular, and no one wanted him hurt, I believe our Dad (the W.W. II fighter pilot) saw my brother's actions as a sign of cowardice.

My brother would have made a great lawyer. He was the best "bull-shitter" I ever knew. Quick-witted, sarcastic, and fast on his feet, he knew just how to cut you (or me) down to size. After two years of law school, he quit under mounting pressure from his longtime girlfriend, "the prom queen" to get married. Dad never forgave him for quitting before taking the bar. For years, my brother struggled to live up to Dad's expectations of him.

Sadly, over time, my brother failed to successfully manage three different dealerships Dad had acquired for him in three different parts of the country. He had become an alcoholic, which he was never able to overcome.

After two failed marriages producing two daughters he ended up alone.

It broke my parents' hearts. The curse of alcoholism which had destroyed my Dad's own family was now devouring his first child's life.

4

BROTHER #2

My second brother was a sickly baby who suffered from convulsions. Mom use to say he was her most difficult child. She spoke of endless nights of walking the floors with a son who cried for hours. Despite ill health, my brother was a survivor. He became a tough kid you didn't mess with. He was the stereotypical Irish hot-head you never crossed. If you did, as I did more than once, you ended up with a fist in the stomach. With #2 there was no in-between – he either loved you or hated you. This brother had no skills for resolving conflicts. That unexpected punch in the gut was all the conflict resolution he needed. The flip side of my brother's Dr. Jekyll and Mr. Hyde personality was a guy who could be vulnerable and sweet who could melt your heart. Sadly we never knew which side of my brother would arrive at the dinner table. We were all kept walking on eggshells for fear of detonating a powder keg.

My second brother was the first of my five brothers, with Dad's help, to become a car dealer. He was a hard worker and became very successful. But something happened along the way that destroyed him. I don't know how or why, but he took his eyes off the ball. He swung at a number of bad pitches. Once power, position, money and eventually corruption came into his life, our fragile relationship had no hope of surviving. While extremely successful my brother bought race cars, racehorses, a helicopter, and enjoyed high stakes gambling. He was living the high life of booze, buxom broads and big business with questionable companions.

Late-night calls from Mom, to me – terror-stricken about "events" happening to her son threatened to destroy everything my parents had built including my Father's sterling reputation.

Since all the principals involved are long dead, I can reveal my brother was involved with others in a scandal involving fraud and racketeering charges which also involved local politicians. Fueled by the media, my brothers' dealership experienced critical press for two solid years. As a result, my brother lost his dealer license, and nearly his freedom. His marriage also ended and, for a time, his relationship with his small children.

While married my brother became involved with a woman with her own history of scrapes with the law. My parents despised "the babe" as Dad referred to her. I hated what she was doing to my parents who spent millions in legal fees to help my brother survive his prosecution problems. By the time my brother's legal nightmare ended "she" had taken command of his life and home – never to let go until the day he died. After vowing NEVER to marry her, he finally did only to discover she cheated on him. He divorced her, but she refused to ever leave his life. To say this woman was obsessed with my brother was an understatement. Once when he dated a beauty queen, "the babe" crashed the party they attended and assaulted his date.

After years of tolerating the offensive behavior of this gold digger, I made the mistake of confronting her – in my own home – for lies she was spreading about my parents. I had finally snapped and told her she wasn't welcome back. My brother sprang to her defense after agreeing WITH ME that "SHE WAS a f_ _ _ _ _ _ liar, but just ignore her." My brother made sure I paid the ultimate price for refusing to subject myself to his girlfriend's scurrilous behavior.

He refused to ever speak to me again.

Looking back, realizing that my brother and his "babe" were alcoholics, this confrontation was inevitable. This woman was the antithesis of everything I stood for all my life. Finally standing up to her, when no one else would, wasn't something I planned, it just happened.

When someone provokes me – in my own home – I'm going to defend myself and my loved ones. And that's what I did.

I loved the "healthy" parts of my brother, but he allowed his "unhealthy" parts to dominate and to bully everyone in his realm. I deserved the respect he was unwilling to show – any woman.

5

BROTHER #3

My third brother was always referred to as the "golden child." Tall, handsome and athletic—good things always seemed to come his way. Since he was close in age to our second brother, the two of them forged a friendship which would last a lifetime. What I remember most growing up was driving him to baseball practice or making cupcakes when his friends were over.

It wasn't until I was in graduate school that I first became aware of a very disturbing pattern in my brother's personality.

As an undergraduate, my brother and I attended the same university. While he was on an athletic scholarship, I was across campus involved in my own activities. We seldom saw each other. About six months into the semester I called home and was berated by Mom for "upsetting" my brother. I had no idea why, neither did Mom. I racked my brain trying to come up with any reason my brother might have had for being so angry with me. I came up with nothing since I had not even seen him on campus for several months. Whatever I had supposedly done, it must have been serious enough to upset our entire family. Months passed with no explanation and no resolution until I got a call from our Mother who had information about the conflict.

A man, who was a family friend of my Dad's, was also friends with my brother's athletic coach. Apparently this man attended numerous athletic practice sessions and witnessed the coach order, my brother, to get a haircut, which ostensibly embarrassed my brother in front of his team and coaches (at that time strict dress codes were enforced at many universities especially for those on scholarships for athletics).

It was proven that my Father's friend had reported to Dad the coach's "hair cut" reprimand involving my brother. Mom conceded I had NOTHING to do with tattle tailing to our Dad what had happened. My brother never apologized for accusing me of something he learned I had no part in.

That was the first time I realized that the men in my family never apologize.

Ever. Looking back I should have seen my brother's insecure, narcissistic tendencies, but I wasn't looking for trouble back then. I was looking toward my own future. So I moved on. In retrospect, I should have paid closer attention.

My brother was only 27 when Dad arranged for him to take charge of his own dealership. Like his older brothers before him, my younger brother began his career on third base but thought he hit a triple in life. Dad's goal of setting all five of his sons up in businesses of their own was coming to fruition and he was proud of giving his third son a chance at the brass ring.

By now my brother had married and had a young family and a new home in the suburbs. They had begun to enjoy all the advantages few of us ever experience, thanks to my folks seed money.

I watched from the sidelines the highs and lows of my brothers' careers as car dealers. If sales were up, Mom and Dad were up. If sales were down, it affected our entire family. Dad had invested millions of His and Mom's money to set their sons up in business, but, besides their enormous financial investments, the emotional toll worried me more. Mom would call me in tears, more times than I could count, telling me that "this son" couldn't meet payroll this month, or "that son" was involved in a lawsuit and needed their help. "Help" always required not just thousands of dollars, but often hundreds of thousands of dollars, or more. Since I wasn't in the car business I had no idea what problems were within my brothers' ability to control and which were beyond their control. I do know my folks began to question the number of vacations taken by one son, or the amount of golf outings by another. Their concern was that the good life was eating up valuable time that should have been dedicated to business matters.

The competition between my brothers intensified over time. Resentments and jealousies ripened into hatred which began to rip the family apart.

I remember one Christmas walking into my brother's living room seeing presents stacked clear to the ceiling for his children alone. Mom couldn't contain her anger when my brother's wife bragged she had gotten all her gifts for "free" from the industries' gift catalog, a perk for earning points during a sales contest. That Christmas she had given my Dad a vinyl garment travel bag. My Mom saw it in the catalog for $20. Hardly an appropriate gift for a Father-in-law who had made her husband a millionaire.

By now I had experienced more than my share of abusive behavior from my 3rd brother. In one instance an F.B.I agent showed up at my brother's front door, unannounced, looking for "Susan." I got an angry call from my brother ordering me to come to his office immediately! When I arrived I was ushered into his office where he slammed the door and asked me if there was "Something" I needed to tell him about? Totally unaware of what he was alluding to, I answered "No." He started screaming at me that his wife had just called him, all upset because the F.B.I had shown up at their house looking for me. I wasn't concerned because I had nothing to be concerned about. My brother interrogated me about drugs until I was nearly in tears. I grew up in the 50s and 60s and never, not even once, did drugs. I never even smoked a cigarette (or anything else).

I was a total square. I never even returned library books late! As it turned out all the agent was interested in was if I knew a man who once was a neighbor of mine in an apartment complex (years before) in another state – across the country. I never knew any of my neighbors back then because I worked long hours at my job, and moved away in a short time. The agent, who was far nicer than my own brother, thanked me for my time and that was all there was to it. End of story.

Reminiscent of the "hair cut" incident at our university decades before, I was accused of a crime, when there was no crime, and convicted for "upsetting his wife" when she had no reason to be overwrought. She certainly showed no concern for me. The incident was never mentioned again, but my brother's reaction began to frighten me.

6

THE FINAL STRAW

The final incident ending our sibling relationship occurred at my brother's dealership many years ago. I had occasional periods in my own career in advertising when work was slow so my brother agreed he could use my help on a part-time basis. This arrangement worked well for over a year.

I made sure my other work never conflicted with the work I did for my brother.

One morning when I arrived for work I noticed my brother's employees staring at me strangely. When I asked why everyone had long faces, fearing someone had died, I was told by a secretary, "Your brother fired you last Friday and announced it to everyone, you don't work here anymore." That's impossible, I thought, my brother would never fire me and announce it publicly without telling me. Shaking from the shock I immediately rushed to his office. Only seconds ahead of me had he left the building, cowardly fleeing to avoid an encounter.

In time I learned his wife was complicit in my firing even though I didn't work for her. Their maid, whom I only knew casually, confronted my brother and his wife after overhearing them plan my demise. She defended me telling her employers, "You don't do that to family! You do not treat your own sister with such disrespect." For attempting to defend me, she lost her job as well.

Four agonizing weeks went by, while I laid on my couch in a fetal position sobbing my eyes out.

Finally, my phone rang and it was my brother's wife wondering "If you had fallen off the face of the earth." "How are you?" She was attempting to make small talk, most likely feeling guilty for her part in my firing. I hung up on her.

I had spent days agonizing over every detail. I attempted to retrace every thought, every word, every step trying to remember anything that I had inadvertently done that may have been construed as hostile or mean. I came up with nothing.

Months turned into years. I was ostracized from their lives and forbidden to see their children whom I adored. In time Mom would question my brother and his wife separately. Their response echoed each other that they had "no problem with Susan." Mom said they couldn't even get their stories straight. One night Mom called me after a late-night call from my younger brother (#4) who was so upset he was in tears. This brother, who was witness to my firing told our Mom, "Susan did nothing wrong." Guilt was eating him alive. Unfortunately for me, this brother was on #3's payroll. He wasn't about to jeopardize his job attempting to seek justice for his sister.

To this day I have no idea what it was I was accused of doing to offend my brother #3.

I was excluded from all family events. My name was to never be mentioned. In time our Father tried to force me to apologize to my brother and his wife. "For what crime?" I asked. For this first—(and only) time in my life, I raised my voice to my Dad. I screamed I would NOT apologize. I told him I never stole any money from my brother, I had never slept with any of his salesmen, that I didn't give a damn if I was the worse employee he ever had, I DESERVED the RESPECT of being told why he fired me.

I yelled at my Father if he wanted to see me swinging from a beam in my barn he could keep up this insanity. I was all done. I had hit a brick wall emotionally.

I was finally finished kissing family asses.

My Father never mentioned the subject again.

You know, if I had been an underachieving bimbo I could have understood my family's treatment.

But that wasn't true. I graduated, on the Dean's List, with my BA from one university, received my master's degree from a different university, and already had a one-man art exhibit at a world famous photographic studio in addition to more than 20 years building my own career – with NO help from "Daddy."

I believed in myself when no one else did. I had more than earned the right to be treated with dignity and honor and I refused to apologize for a "mythical" offense that never happened.

Do we see a pattern of behavior in brother #3?

In time, circumstances would give my brother and his (estranged) wife their best shot at bringing me down.

My fight was long from over.

7

BROTHER #4

My fourth brother was a sweet child who always had a serious, worried look on his face. He had a quiet nature in contrast to his twin sister whose boisterous personality overshadowed him. He was a follower all his life and seemed resigned to do so. Once he came of age he worked at his older brothers' dealerships patiently learning all he could until it was his turn to run his own store.

While his professional life seemed on track, his private life had run off the rails. He got involved with a woman he told me he did not love, got her pregnant and ended up marrying her after she was eight months pregnant with their second child. Mom and Dad kept their shame and disappointment inside and hoped a dealership of his own would help their fourth son get his life back on track. Unfortunately my brother's marriage was doomed from the start. His wife had a cocaine habit and became an exotic dancer. It was a terrible time for a young Father who was trying to establish his new business as well as worry about his children's needs.

In what can only be described as my brother's incessant bad luck, the scandal which enveloped his older brother in a neighboring city, predisposed this young dealer to so much bad publicity (with same name recognition), he was forced to close his doors. He lost everything. This contributed to our parents' depression as the fall-out of one son's mistakes had abruptly taken its toll on another son's future.

It was inevitable my brother's marriage would end. Compounded by the pain of another divorce in our very "Catholic" family, my parents were shocked their son had taken up with his ex-wife's best friend. Mom referred to this new girlfriend as "the biker babe" whose ex-husband was in prison. Looking back I've come to believe my brother never thought he deserved better than he got in his choice of women. Reaching for fruit a little higher on the tree rather than settling for fruit that had fallen to the ground would have made all the difference in his life. This brother's troubles were often self-induced.

I always felt sorry for my fourth brother, whether by circumstances beyond his control or his own poor choices, it broke my heart to see him suffering. I remember sending him $1,000 after he told me he had holes in his shoes as well as his children's.

Predictably, his second marriage floundered with the addition of three more children after his first two resented their new stepmother.

Heavily influenced and on the payroll of brother #3 it was only a matter of time before my once sweet, vulnerable brother turned into a man I no longer recognized or respected. It didn't take long before we couldn't find much to talk about.

It makes me sad to think of him. I'll never understand why people lower their standards believing life will somehow be easier. It seldom happens that way.

I always believed my fourth brother had great potential until I grew older and learned that anyone with great potential is already using it.

8

MY SISTER

I remember the day Dad told me I had a new baby brother. # 4. I was heartbroken. I had wanted a sister in the worse way. His news made me cry. I already had three brothers, and now a fourth? By the time Dad convinced me I would learn to love him, my Father could no longer contain his joy and announced Mom had ALSO had a baby girl. Twins? Yes, twins! I can live with that. The eight and a third years age difference between us was not something I considered when I put in my order for a "buddy" sister. I never counted on the fact that, to my sister, I was just another Mother, a surrogate she wanted no part of.

As we grew my sister and I were continually compared to our Mom and her sister, who were total opposites. Mom was a refined lady. A girlie girl always perfectly groomed. Our aunt was gregarious, sassy, messy, and confident. I took after Mom. My sister, our aunt. There was no way my sister and I would ever become great friends. Not only were our personalities different, we came from different generations. As the older daughter, I was held to a higher, almost impossible, standard, while my baby sister got away with everything.

I was away at college when my sister was still in grade school. Time and distance only widened the gap between us. Sadly, we didn't share the same ethics, morals or values. I grew up fearing our Dad. I lived dreading the time I might get "the look" from my Father for doing something wrong. On the other hand my sister didn't give a damn. Her rationalism was "If Dad's mad, that's HIS problem, not mine."

Ironically, my aunt and I were very close despite our differences. She was my godmother. I was the "daughter" she never had after having three sons.

To illustrate a point about my sister, my aunt used to tell a story, my Mother corroborated, when my sister was a teenager. One morning, while visiting our family, my aunt was enjoying a cup of morning coffee with my Father, who was always an early riser, when my sister burst into the kitchen with a cigarette dangling from her mouth. Dad, who never smoked, asked my sister if she would please NOT smoke in the house.

My sister took a long drag, walked over to my Dad, and exhaled right in his face. She then poured herself a cup of coffee and left without saying a word.

"What was that?" my aunt asked. "My hostile, impertinent youngest daughter who doesn't know the meaning of the word, respect," Dad answered.

I was furious at my sister for her blatant display of hostility towards our Dad who was entitled to make a simple request in his home.

By the time I had completed college as well as graduate school and moved into my first apartment, my sister had already flunked out of college. She told me once she hated me for, as she put it, "being the perfect daughter." I was/and am—FAR from perfect, but I didn't know what my sister expected of me. What was I supposed to do? Underachieve to make her feel better about having lower standards and goals in life? I had no chance of winning that battle, so I never tried.

As with my other siblings, my sister was someone I distanced myself from most of my adult life, not because I wanted to, but because I had to.

When my sister became involved with a married man, whose marriage ended as a result, she landed a direct hit to my heart when she married the guy and asked a girlfriend to be her maid of honor and not her only sister. I resented every moment of that "event" because my sister deliberately intended to humiliate me, and she did. To add fuel to the fire our parents forced me to assume the role of lowly bridesmaid while my sister's friend flaunted her status as maid of honor. In time I was to learn (from Mom) my sister had had a falling out with her maid of honor, and they never spoke again. Welcome to my world, honey!

My sister's descent into unbridled alcoholism was tragic to witness. A cousin who saw her, told me she had lost all her teeth and had developed a serious heart problem which was deemed, "Susan's fault."

I can only assume it was also my fault her husband divorced her for another woman. What goes around…

My sister was once a pretty daughter. She was athletic and vivacious and fun when she was sober. Tragically, I rarely saw her lucid. I wasn't the only family member who cowered once her vitriolic remarks cut you down to size and embarrassed our refined parents.

I wish I could have helped her, but, she made it clear, even as a child, she never wanted my help. I remember my little sister, and her twin brother best as little children ready for bed in their "bunnies" (the jammies with feet), my sister in pink, her twin in blue.

How adorable they were – warm and cuddly. Those are my happiest memories of the twins.

9

MY BABY, BROTHER #5

Mom had two-year-old twins on her hands when her youngest was born. From the moment Mom placed him in my ten-year-old arms I adored my baby brother. He was adorable.

Once in grammar school he was assigned to write a paper on his family. He started with Dad, then Mom, then proceeded to describe all of his siblings, describing each by their characteristics that made the biggest impression on him. Though I was second in birth order, my brother had me last on his list. At the bottom of the page, my brother had printed "Susan. She raised me." Mom got a kick out of that joking, "Where the hell was I?" Everyone knew my youngest brother and I had a special bond; a bond I could have sworn would never be broken.

Brother #5 learned by watching the mistakes his older siblings made. Quiet and gentle, he shared my love for animals. His relaxed demeanor attracted critters repelled by the often vociferous brothers. He told me things I never shared with anyone else. I never betrayed his trust. My youngest brother watched our Dad launch his older sons into the auto business. Once the scandals, lawsuits, and divorces began, Dad's closest confidant became his youngest son. Dad trusted his fifth and final son who became his protégé. It was our Dad's choice to make this son executor of his and Mom's estate, bypassing his four older sons.

My youngest brother use to say Dad chose him because he hadn't lived long enough to screw up his life as his older brother's had.

Sadly, one day he would.

When my fifth brother took a wife, I had hopes of being a favorite aunt once his twins came along. They had moved across the country after Dad installed him in a dealership, family-owned, which was on life support after brother #1 had failed to make a go of it. As long as Dad was running the show, hope of turning things around prevailed. But that could not be sustained forever.

Once my brother lost his coach and mentor, it was only a matter of time before disaster struck.

In the meantime, my fifth brother bought a new house with a pool for his young family and seemed happy in his new life. After one visit I was shocked to discover his wife to be a spoiled and lazy "princess" who believed she hit the lotto in life marrying automotive money. This young woman was young enough to be my daughter. Like many from her generation, she showed little respect for me despite my affection for her husband. In time when she didn't get her way, she would prove to be an immature, vindictive brat, who, like previous "wives" would help destroy my relationship with my brother.

I was raised to play by the rules, and I did. It wasn't even in my DNA to cause trouble or be disrespectful to my brothers, especially once they had wives and children. I never made any demands. I had no reason to. I loved my family especially since I wasn't blessed with one of my own. I was the most accomplished woman in my family, with more degrees and professional experience under my belt than all the others. Still, I was never able to attain the respect afforded by my brother's wives because I was not married. I never understood why, maybe it was simple maturity. I was the only woman in my family who had to work for a living and, as such, I didn't have time (or interest) in laying around watching TV all day in my pajamas. I had clients, employees, and deadlines to meet. Beyond that, I ran my ranch. I simply didn't have time for Jerry Springer or Oprah.

Nevertheless I was respectful and only stood my ground after I was backed into a corner.

One such "corner" came after Dad's death when an adjoining farm to mine became available and, after a two-year struggle to stop a greedy developer from putting up 730 tract houses, I convinced Mom this was a great investment. Mom bought the farm. My youngest brother, acting as her executor, completed the transaction. I had done all of the leg work.

Before the ink was dry on the contract, my brother's 20 something wife had secretly decided to install her younger sister and her live-in boyfriend on the farm.

Neither my brother's wife, who lived across the country, nor her sister had even seen the property, nor had they attended even one town hall meeting in a two-year period to squelch the development. I alone had been the only family member involved in the two-year battle.

When I objected to my sister-in-law's attempt to take control of this property for HER own families use Mom agreed with me, and stopped her dead in the tracks.

That was the beginning of the end for me. My brother, who gave no indication to Mom or me he had turned this property over to his wife, turned on me like a rabid dog. Our Mother was furious her youngest son had acted with no regard to her wishes. She was more infuriated her daughter-in-law attempted to take control of Mom's asset behind her back.

My brother's wife never forgave me for intervening in her selfish plan.

My brother launched more than one plan to get even with me.

The gloves were off, he had gone over to the dark side. My baby brother, whom I regarded as my closest ally cut me out of his life.

Decades after my brother (#5) turned on me I am still shocked in the total transformation in his character.

Clearly, his immature wife contributed to his downfall, but that only happened because he allowed himself to be controlled by her selfish demands.

Something deeper was happening within.

What I did know was that none of my brothers had ever had to get a real job on their own. All five sons were handed a variety of positions directly as a result of my Dad's high position in the corporation. Once you have a safety net with very deep pockets you begin to arrogantly believe your infallible. Reality, as most of us know it, becomes distorted.

What I did learn was one way or another, everyone pays a price in life, either early on, or down the road. No one is immune.

10

SUSAN

When I was five years old, my parents lived back east in a suburb in the first real home I could remember. Our house was on a corner lot in a new area with lots of young families. It was the early fifties. One day I got invited to a little friend's birthday party in the neighborhood. The girl lived across the street from me. I was too young to recall the exact arrangements except that we were to dress very casual in our dungarees (as jeans were called back then). All week I looked forward to the party and Mom let me help her wrap a pretty present for my friend. The morning of the celebration I was walked across the street.

I was ushered inside and my escort promptly left. When I walked into the living room I was shocked to see ten other little girls all dressed up in their best, most frilly, lacy pastel party dresses. Unable to move, I stood frozen holding the gift. Finally, the birthday girl greeted me by saying, "Is that for me?" As I handed her the present, I overheard an adult say they must have forgotten to call my Mom about the change in plans from casual to party dresses. Someone else said, "She's here now, it doesn't matter what she's wearing. It's okay." But it was NOT okay. The pain of how awful it felt that day to be different tagged me all my life. Here were all these beautiful princesses and I walked in, the ugly duckling in jeans. I was too little to speak up. Someone should have walked me home and had my Mother doll me up in a party dress, but no one did. Because I felt so out of place, I had a terrible time. It sounds silly and shallow to an adult, but to a little girl of five back in the 1950s, a party dress and a pair of Mary Jane's was your life's ambition.

Little did I know that this "party dress" story would become a metaphor for my life.

I didn't know then that my gender and birth order would cast me in a role I could never escape. I was only eight but perceptive enough to notice the concerned look on my Daddy's face. He told me that Mommy was very sick and he needed me to help him with the chores as well as my brothers. As is common between little girls and their Fathers, I adored my Daddy. He only had to ask me once for help. From that moment on – I became the compliant "good girl." I became the child Mom and Dad could really depend on. More than my role in our growing Irish Catholic family, it became my calling. If they needed a cook, I cooked. If they needed a housekeeper, I cleaned. If they needed a sitter, I babysat. Because my parent's needed my help, as the oldest daughter, I believed, back then, that my highest calling was to serve the needs of my family. Fueled by my Catholic school education I never said no and never rebelled. I did what I was asked to do because I believed I was honoring my Mother and Father. As the years passed and more children came along, I became the "go-to" kid who could be counted on for almost anything.

I proudly watched my Father work his way up the automotive corporate ladder. Unfortunately, I often had to watch from afar because Dad traveled constantly, which meant he left Mom at home to raise the children, for the most part – alone, that's why he asked me to help her. I willingly obliged and did all that I could to make things at home go as smoothly as possible. Looking back, I had an enormous responsibility for a child.

As Dad's positions got bigger, my own duties grew when Mom was expected to accompany him on many trips around the country and world.

When it came to my folks, I played things pretty straight. Though I came of age smack in the middle of the 60s, I was fairly conservative. Most adults found I was mature and responsible. I had earned my parent's respect and trust and that meant everything to me.

I was an old fashioned girl who loved horses and romantic Broadway musicals. I thought drugs and alcohol were stupid (I still do).

I adored my successful parents. They more than deserved the rewards they worked so hard to achieve. None of my girlfriend's Fathers were on local TV or made the cover of industry magazines, spoke at the White House, flew in corporate jets, or attended elegant functions in chauffeured limousines with such entertainment giants as Bob Hope or Paul Newman.

Deep down, I knew I would never live that kind of life, but I was content to live vicariously through Mom and Dad.

My set of standards came from my parent's generation, not my own. I was twelve when I remember thinking that if I ever lost my parents and had to look at them in their coffins I wanted to have no regrets, no guilt, and no doubts that I had done my best to be a good daughter. I always tried hard to please. I was tough on myself. It was my job to please others, and, when I couldn't, I felt inadequate.

Whenever I had time to myself, I daydreamed about living the country life with horses and lots of animals. I started riding at age twelve, and by thirteen I was jumping four-foot fences. At sixteen I was asked to teach riding.

Most of my girlfriends forgot about horses when they reached puberty and discovered boys. Not me. After growing up in a household with six men, I was willing to postpone that "hobby" for a while.

While still in grammar school the nuns noticed my budding artistic talent after embellishing my school assignments. By the time I graduated from high school, everyone assumed I would become an artist. I was labeled "Susan the artist." I was cast as a bit of a misfit, a freak. I already knew artists seldom got rich and women rarely made more money than men, no matter their profession. However, I felt that my creative abilities were a God-given gift I had a special obligation to pursue.

My goals were not dissimilar to the majority of women in my generation—education, career, marriage, then Motherhood. I set out to prepare myself for the most important job a woman could have, based on my sheltered, naïve upbringing, that of wife and Mother. I already knew how to cook, clean, sew, and take care of children. A good education and some career experience would make me a great candidate for marriage when the time came. Or so I thought.

As I pursued my college education, I saw a world I never knew existed. The "hippie" revolution was in full swing. Janis Joplin and the Stones had arrived and relegated Sandra Dee and Frankie Avalon to the fading fifties. Sex, drugs, and booze were as available as the soft drinks in the vending machine down the hall in my dorm.

Between semesters of college, I worked at a fabulous commercial photographic studio as an apprentice "photo stylist" under the tutelage of an elegant older man who knew antiques, fashion, decorating and became my lifelong friend as well as my mentor. He appreciated my creative talents and hard work ethic and introduced me to the world of high-fashion, food styling, product display, art, and antiques. As an eighteen-year-old I flourished around this group of imaginative, highly talented professionals.

It was the first time I felt recognized, not only for my talent, but they found me fun and funny, something I was never allowed to be at home.

It was the best job I ever had.

After earning my BA, I went on to pursue a master's degree to silence my skeptics who saw an art degree (with minors in Philosophy and English) as an inferior education. I applied, and was accepted, to one school where I would be forced to compete one-on-one with men, an all-male university (at that time very few women were admitted and ONLY at the graduate level).

All my life people seemed to underestimate me. Ending my formal education at such a prestigious institution would certainly silence my critics, or so I hoped.

By my early twenties I was working independently of my family for my own American Dream. After college, I worked autonomously as a photographic set designer, photo stylist, interior designer, artist, illustrator, and part-time college art professor. I had my hands full.

Over two decades I built my career by working for others in three major cities, north, south and west. A few times Dad would offer to help me get my own studio, but I always said "No thanks." I never felt ready. I was grateful he asked.

The last fifteen years of my career I landed an important part of one of the most successful catalogs in the industry. I was very happy both Mom and Dad lived to see me succeed in my profession. That meant the world to me.

By the time I reached my thirties, I still had not married. My folks, who had helped all six of my siblings jump-start their lives with jobs, incredible career opportunities, new homes, and expensive weddings (which for the most part, they paid for) wanted some security for me.

That was when I got the call from Dad to my tiny apartment, to begin looking for a ranch out West, where he grew up. After a two-year hunt I found a ranch Dad and Mom wanted to buy for me. My Mother's direct quote to me was, "We bought the dealerships for the (five) boys, we're buying the ranch for Susie."

What was never spoken, but definitely implied, was that the ranch was their gift to me for sacrificing my childhood to help them raise their children. It was their most generous nod to me in appreciation for decades of love and devotion to the family.

It was NOT a business arrangement. No rent was expected. My Father, who had once met President John F. Kennedy, was enamored with the "Kennedy Compound" on Cape Cod and envisioned a similar complex (out West) for his family.

I welcomed that idea. With no family of my own, I relished the thought of sharing the country life with family, I had been alone for too long.

So I made the ranch my home for the next twenty years.

It never occurred to me to worry that I would ever have to leave my home. My parents both let me know they had taken "legal steps" to protect me down the road.

I knew Dad had a fifty-one percent interest in some of "his" dealerships while he outwardly owned others. He was a brilliant businessman.

I trusted my parents. They had my best interests at stake. I had security.

But how long would it last?

PART TWO

The Nightmare Begins

11

COMING APART AT THE SEAMS

Not long after I settled in at the ranch my family started coming apart at the seams. My third brother and his wife were involved in separations, my second brother divorced after having two children. Brother number one divorced after having one child and brother number four had gotten a girl pregnant and had to get married. My sister, involved with a married man, planned to marry out of the Church, once his divorce came through which broke my devoted Father's heart.

In time #1 would remarry and divorce again. #2 would also remarry and divorce. #3, #5, as well as my sister, would all divorce. The one brother who did not divorce had a long history of affairs and wasn't about to share his assets with his "estranged" wife.

To say this marital track record destroyed my parents is an understatement.

Mom use to tell me, "I think you're the smart one, Susan, for never marrying."

Hard times test us, not easy times. Emerging events would reveal my brothers' abilities to demonstrate their business proficiencies.

One by one the dominoes began to fall.

12

LOSING DAD

When Mom called to tell me Dad was dying, I could not believe it. Dad knew for four years before he was forced to tell the love of his life he was terminally ill with leukemia. He swore Mom to secrecy, but time was running out.

I couldn't find the right words to console my Mother because I realized my world would never be the same. The fear I had always dreaded with the passing of our patriarch was now gripping my heart and wouldn't let go.

How would our family survive without Dad?

In the few remaining weeks of my Dad's life, he felt well enough to celebrate his and Mom's fiftieth wedding anniversary. They wanted to renew their wedding vows at a special Mass attended by all their children and extended family.

During the church service when Dad repeated his vows to Mom, "in sickness and in health", I could no longer hold back my tears. I couldn't catch my breath, I was heartbroken.

Because of the estrangement from my siblings, I had no one to turn to for comfort.

Two weeks later Mom called telling me Dad had been hospitalized. I knew the end was coming so I flew cross country to be with Dad and help Mom in any way I could. My parent's condo was congested with family members so I slept on the floor of Mom's walk-in closet (which I joked was bigger than most of the apartments I ever had).

It was Christmas time and the beautiful new hospital Dad was in had a live stream in the lobby with an impressive black baby grand piano that was programmed to play Christmas carols. As difficult as it was to watch my Dad dying little by little, those final days with him meant the world to me. Even in dying, my handsome Dad conducted himself with great courage and dignity.

One night when the nurses were busy helping other patients, I changed my Father's diapers. Halfway through the process, a nurse appeared. "Where are your rubber gloves?" she asked, attempting to make the task easier for me. I answered, "He changed plenty of my diapers when I was a baby and HE never wore gloves."

Mom was shocked at my ability to weather the hospital duties I had taken on myself, knowing I had the weakest stomach in any medical setting. I used to say I thought God put me on 'auto-pilot' to help me through those emotionally draining days.

One night at Mom's condo while everyone was asleep, and Dad was nearing the end of his life, I sat at the dining room table alone in silence. My second brother, the hothead, came in and sat down. He began to talk to me respectfully, as he never had before. I had learned from years on the ranch how to deal with a frightened or injured animal and I knew my brother was a very injured soul.

I sat still and quiet and let him talk.

"You know Dad's dying?" he opened. I nodded and started to cry. I knew he was right, but I didn't want to hear it.

"You know I've really screwed up my life."

What an admission. It was as close to an apology as he'd ever come.

"I lived in the fast lane for a long time, but I don't do that anymore. It ain't worth it. It doesn't mean shit. It didn't make me happy. Now #3 is living the life I used to live: the babes, the booze, the bucks."

His confession of a hedonistic lifestyle didn't shock me. Both brothers had made millions of dollars thanks to Mom and Dad, but #2 was speaking as a broken, defeated man. It was very sad.

He continued, "#3 doesn't realize the fast track he is on leads to nowhere. But he will have to learn the hard way, 'cause he ain't listening to me."

I wanted to tell my brother how much I respected his talking to me, but I dared not. I wanted to hug him, too, but I held back. I knew what an injured, frightened animal was capable of and I didn't want to press my luck.

The last hours of Dad's life were over Christmas. All my siblings left to spend the holiday with their families. I had no other family, therefore it was easy for them to fall back on their old thinking from our childhood: "Susan doesn't have any needs. She's here to serve our needs."

I was left alone, splitting my time between Dad at the hospital and Mom alone at the condo. Mom was having a major meltdown at home while I was waiting to talk to Dad's doctor about how much time my Father had left. I desperately needed someone to lean on, but there was no one.

On Christmas morning the hospital chaplain came into Dad's room to administer Holy Communion to Dad and to me. Dad had slipped into a coma and could not swallow the Host. This was my Dad's last Christmas on earth. This was the last time Dad and I would share in the sacraments together. I held Dad's hand tight. As the priest blessed Dad then left, the doctor arrived.

"I need you to level with me," I said. "How much time does my Dad have left?"

"Forty-eight hours," he said.

Mom would get her wish. Dad would not die on Christmas day.

On December 27, 1994, while I sat at his bedside still holding his hand, my Father drew his last breath. His end came quickly. I remember praying, "Lord, Please welcome him into your kingdom."

My older brother (#1) who sat in a chair in Dad's hospital room began ordering me around, telling me to get a nurse. Realizing that my Father's final seconds on earth were fleeting by I decided it was most important to thank him for all he did for us. So I began shouting to my dying Father, "Thanks Dad for everything, we all love you. Thanks, Dad."

Eventually, my brother joined me in saying "thank you, thank you" over and over again until a nurse arrived and said, "He's gone."

I dissolved in tears, but my brother did not speak to me or offer any comfort. No hug. Nothing. I walked out of the room. A priest friend, and three nuns were waiting outside the door. "He's gone," I said. My knees buckled and the nuns grabbed me and led me to the hospital waiting room so Father could bless Dad's lifeless body. One of the nun's asked, "Susan, do you know that your Father just bestowed on you a great honor?"

"The person dying always decides who they want to be with them at the end. Your Dad chose you." I wasn't sure I believed this nun, but I appreciated her efforts to comfort me. I will forever be grateful that I was with my beloved Father at the moment of his passing. I believe in some way that I handed him over to Almighty God. A very humbling experience to contemplate.

Years after Dad's death, my brother circulated the story that he ALONE was with our Dad when he died. Despite the witnesses who could easily corroborate the truth, I never confronted my brother. I thought this obvious attempt to achieve some sort of self-importance was pathetic. Dad knows I was there—that's all that matters to me.

Dad's funeral was scheduled for New Year's Eve, the day before his birthday. The night Dad died I began writing his eulogy. I told no one for fear of recrimination.

I was helping Mom get ready for the "viewing" the night prior to Dad's funeral by doing her hair as I had done for important occasions for over thirty years. When the phone rang Mom answered it since she was receiving so many condolence calls from around the country.

The call was from brother (son) #3 wondering if he, and his brothers, were "obligated" to dress up for this "thing" tonight?

"This thing," Mom said, "is the public viewing of your Father lying in his coffin."

You would think his sons would have had enough respect to honor their Father by dressing up for his funeral.

Mom was seething with anger—with good reason.

The morning of Dad's funeral, I wondered if the eulogy I had written for Dad would be read by my Father's priest friend. Once the service began, the archdiocesan Bishop reached into his pocket and announced, "I could not have written anything better to eulogize my friend. This is a letter from his daughter Susan."

The Bishop slowly and carefully delivered my eulogy for Dad. I got goosebumps. It was the proudest moment of my life.

A Letter From Daughter Susan to Her Dad

My Dearest, beloved Father,

These last two weeks we spent together have been the two most incredible weeks of my life. Even in dying you taught me more about living and about loving than I could have ever imagined possible. I know I speak for all of us, your beloved children, in saying Thank You.

Thank you for the countless times you held our hands when we were sick, or when we felt the pain of rejection. We never knew then that you felt our pain one hundred times worse.

Thank you for all the advantages you gave us, advantages few people ever had.

Thank you for the countless hours you worked to provide us with the best education.

Thank you for believing in our abilities and in our potential often when we didn't believe in ourselves.

Thank you for your wonderful sense of humor, hearing your laugh was the most beautiful music any of us could ever imagine.

Thank you for sharing your deepest devotion of all: your devotion to the Blessed Virgin Mary and her Most Precious Son.

And finally, thank you for our Mother. Your love story will be told for generations to come.

No one else has ever come close to the kind of man my Father was. Dad, you set the standards—for husbands, for brothers, for sons, for friends, for Fathers. How privileged we were to have had you as our Father and how honored we were to have had you as our friend. Our hearts are broken, but your heavenly love, and the love of our Holy Mother Mary, will sustain us until we are with you again. I love you forever.

Your daughter,
Susan

*****

Mom was so proud of what I wrote for Dad that she asked me for copies of the eulogy so she could include it with all her responses to condolence letters. She also asked me when her time came if I would honor her with a eulogy "just the way I had Dad." I never told anyone of Mom's request for fear of further reprisal from my bitter siblings.

13

THE BLACK BOOKS

Dad had known for some time that the form of leukemia he had was fatal. He prepared his estate as a trust leaving everything to Mom. Intending to instruct her after his death, Dad put all the information she would need in two black binder books. One book recorded every asset of the estate including huge sums of money owed to the estate by my brothers. The second black book entailed what to do with everything including stocks, deeds, properties, cash, etc… I never saw the black books, but I knew they existed because Dad and Mom both told me about them. Let me repeat the fact that I NEVER saw the black books.

The day Dad died my Mother returned from the hospital to her condo to discover two of her sons ravaging through legal files. It was #2 and #3. They retreated quickly when I approached with my aunt, Mom's sister, to work on funeral arrangements. When she opened the door we were greeted with Mom sobbing, "They stole my Black Books, my sons (#2 & #3) stole my Black Books." She was inconsolable. Everything she needed to know about her estate estimated at around thirty million dollars was recorded in those Black Books, and now they were gone. NOT misfiled, NOT misplaced, but stolen by her own sons in a premeditated attempt to change the power structure from Mom to her sons, whom Dad never trusted. It didn't take Sherlock Holmes to figure out who had the most to gain from stealing the black books. All you had to do was look at motive.

Who owed Dad and Mom the most money? Stealing Dad's records made it impossible for Mom to ever recover millions of dollars in debts owed her by her own sons. At the time of Dad's death, brother #5 assumed the role of executor. He seemed the perfect choice. He had all the requirements for the job: brains, Dad's respect and trust, and yes, he was male (no man in Dad's generation—deep-seeded in chauvinism, would have ever appointed a daughter as executor).

Both my parents had wills/trusts for the distribution of their assets. Dad had a team of CPAs, estate planners, tax specialists, attorneys in several states as well as the large Midwest bank he hired as co-trustee whose job it was to insure the fair and honest disbursement of his and Mom's assets. A checks and balances set up to prevent any one (or more) of their heirs from stealing from the others.

Once Dad was gone—so was their loyalty. One by one the "team" of men charged with handling estate matters for my folks began shifting their allegiance to my brothers. In my opinion, what they did was not only immoral and unethical, it was illegal. Once the Black Books "disappeared" Mom knew her sons were already stealing from her.

Important point to remember:

When someone is hell-bent on stealing from their elderly or dying parent— the stealing begins long BEFORE the parent dies.

These people are predators—they have enormous power because they are not constrained by morals or values or love. They don't care who they destroy in the process. They see an easy opportunity to steal, and they go for it.

Stealing Dad's Black Books was my brothers' preemptive strike against everyone in our family, especially our Mother.

It signified the end of my parent's dream for their family. It marked the beginning of the end of their legacy, and Mom knew it.

14

WRESTLING FOR THE WHEEL OF THE TITANIC

As the first year anniversary of Dad's death came around, Mom was happy her eldest son would be joining her for the holidays. My oldest brother had a serious problem with alcohol all his adult life. Before Dad died, he agreed to pay for my brother to go to a substance abuse facility. I remember Mom telling me the cost was $27,000 for the four-week treatment program. Once completed Mom believed her eldest son was sober. What she didn't know was my brother had left "drunk school", as he called it, after only two weeks.

As Christmas approached Mom put up decorations and planned to prepare her family food favorites. She also invited a friend who was a manager at Mom's bank, an elderly woman to share her holiday.

Christmas morning Mom called me sobbing. My brother had failed to show up the previous night as planned. When he finally did, he was drunk. He and Mom had a heated argument. She retreated to her bedroom for privacy and locked the door.

She called her banker friend and canceled Christmas dinner. She spent Christmas day in tears. The following day Mom called to tell me my brother had left, but not before stopping by Mom's bank in an attempt to withdraw $350,000 from her bank account. His feeble attempt at extortion failed. #1 had aligned himself with his youngest brother, #5 who had already made a number of mistakes as executor. Mom's trust in him was failing. These missteps opened the door just wide enough to let brother #2 inside along with his sidekicks, #3 and #4. Mom's hothead, volatile, prodigal son had returned after his estrangement following the "Black Books" incident. Mom feared this son. We ALL did. You didn't cross him. He loved wielding fear as a means of achieving power. He was bone thin at 6'4. At one point Mom thought he had gotten AIDS from his second wife who slept around. Mom had a new project, first, to help restore #2's health by making all his favorite meals, and second, to fire her youngest son (once appointed by Dad) as executor. This plan was very carefully orchestrated. It did, however, create a hell of a mess because son #5 still retained a fair amount of legal power. They had secured many legal documents, including deeds, and they controlled the family partnership. My brother (#5) and his cronies (legal team) still had access to millions of Mom's money.

Though #2 believed he was Mom's "knight" come to save the day, everyone knows that armor rusts in salt air. Mom had given control of her estate to the captain of the Titanic and the iceberg was only months away.

Once Dad was gone, I watched all five of my brothers jockey for position of executor. They had formed alliances with attorneys who were supposed to act impartially in the best interest of ALL the beneficiaries, not just the sons.

Smart enough to realize my own interests would never be respected by any configuration of my brothers (since they clearly had no respect for women), I hired a local attorney to protect me from losing what I cherished most, my ranch.

It had been my home for two decades.

Coincidentally, there was a young, 21-year-old woman (from the same county my Irish relatives came from) on board at the "Titanic", with my same family name. She was coming to America for her American Dream.

She was never found and was presumed to have gone down with the ship.

I was beginning to worry I would suffer a similar fate.

15

THE IN-LAWS

Mom attributed a lot of our family problems to what she called "greedy gold-digging in-laws." Not in every case, but certainly in most instances, Mom was right. None of us seven kids had fortunes of our own. Principally, it was Mom and Dad's money. Over time Mom and Dad became disgusted with their sons' wives' lack of gratefulness. Because my eight sisters-in-law and one brother-in-law only saw the fruits of my parents' fifty-year struggle, they were oblivious to the enormous sacrifices my folks had made to ensure a more secure, less Spartan future for their seven children. Still, that was no excuse for the arrogance and feeling of entitlement that the in-laws garnered when they entered the realm of my family.

One of the most obvious examples involved dinner plans at upscale restaurants where Dad was invariably left with the check. No one thought twice about this and of course my Dad would never say anything. Dad didn't have a selfish bone in his body and for years everyone took advantage of his generosity. In private, though, Mom would tell me (the kid with no in-laws) how hurt she and Dad were. They took notice when daughters-in-law at upscale restaurants would order the most expensive things on the menu at Dad's expense: Oysters Rockefeller, Clams on the Half Shell, Lobster, and Chateaubriand, along with aperitifs, mixed drinks, cordials. It was always expected that Dad would pay and he always did.

Mom was especially peeved with my sister's husband who never once picked up a check when my folks were around. It became a hurtful family joke. He apologized one time, claiming he forgot his credit card, and offered, "I'll pay next time, Dad." That time never came. "Forgot his credit card, my patootie", Mom said. "He's just cheap!" My brother-in-law never once treated my parents to a cup of coffee.

Mom and I discussed the in-law situation so many times that it became one of our major topics of conversation. Mom used to say, "Susan, we never had family problems 'til we got in-laws." I agreed.

In the beginning, I only had one criterion for judging the spouses of my siblings: how they treated my siblings. It was that simple. Once children came along, they were added to my rule. If the in-laws treated their spouses and children respectfully, they were okay in my book.

Later, however, when I saw the havoc wreaked on our family because of the interference by in-laws, I changed my mind. Maybe because I never married I developed a strong stance on this subject. When someone marries into money belonging to his or her spouse's parents, it is just that, THEIR SPOUSE'S PARENTS' MONEY, NOT THEIRS. Unless someone has earned the money him or herself, it does not belong to them. Marrying into money does not make it theirs.

It never ceased to amaze me that whenever I encountered arrogance in people, that without exception, most of them have achieved very little on their own. Arrogance is the opposite of humility. Arrogance is being proud of something not earned. When someone benefits from marrying into a family with money, they tend to think they have hit life's lottery. Nothing could be further from the truth. Unless someone has the character and the humility to appreciate the genuine sacrifices others have made for his or her benefit, that person sets themselves up to become a Prima Donna.

Unfortunately, most people want something for nothing. At whose expense?

When my brothers married and introduced their wives into the family, Mom took a stance about in-laws in matters she valued most. She was not a timid, shrinking violet when it came to issues dear to her heart. Mom's jewelry was one of those matters. Mom wanted her jewelry to go ONLY to her two daughters NOT to her eight daughters-in-law or to her granddaughters who were deliberately excluded from her will. Mom believed in the old saying: "A son is a son until he takes a wife, but a daughter is a daughter for the rest of her life."

More than once a daughter-in-law would covet Mom's precious jewelry and not hesitate to point to a ring on Mom's hand or a bracelet on her wrist and say, "I want that when you die." That arrogance made Mom's skin crawl. While she was extremely kind and generous to all of her children and their spouses, she still felt that they had no right to assume that one day they would get first pick over anything she owned.

When Mom's sons divorced and their ex-wives took "everything" with them, Mom felt even stronger in her convictions. "See, Susan, once the boys divorce, anything given to their wives, leaves with the wives. I don't want my personal things going to my sons' wives." Mom made herself clear and her sons knew it… so did their wives.

*****

I don't believe "in-laws" have the right to interfere in family estate issues. That doesn't mean they won't. Remember: It is NOT their parents' money. They never saw the countless sacrifices made in order to build a family and an estate. Those who feel entitled simply by reason of marrying into a family do not care about anyone's wishes but their own. They only care about the money.

The most powerful weapon greedy in-laws have in getting what they want is control over their spouse and children. Using their own children to punish others is a time-honored tradition. Greedy in-laws will use their children as weapons in punitive retaliation against their spouse or their spouse's parents. It's called emotional blackmail.

This certainly happened to my parents. When in-laws used grandchildren to hurt grandparents that only made my parents more determined to leave their estate ONLY to their own seven children. This need for control and this false sense of entitlement by many in-laws was a major contributing factor to the failure of my parent's immense estate plan. Grateful and loving in-laws are not greedy. They do not steal. And they do not covet what does not belong to them. THE MARRIAGE LICENSE IS NOT MEANT TO BE A LICENSE TO STEAL. If my parents had had a grateful, instead of greedy, son-in-law and daughters-in-law, our family would have been much better off. My parents were wary. They tried to take the necessary steps to address this issue when preparing their wills. Still, they underestimated the influence and power that spouses had over their sons and daughter.

It makes one wonder how many married into my family for the money? All you had to do was look at the divorce rate to wonder…

16

DAD'S DYING WISH

Before his death, while my Father was, literally, on his deathbed he told me, as well as my Mother, that it was his wish that we build a studio at my ranch for my advertising work. I was appreciative and Mom agreed it would give me something to look forward to after losing my beloved Father.

Mom faced fierce opposition from three of my brothers, (#1, #2 and #3) about helping me fulfill Dad's dying wish for his daughter. My punitive brothers hoped I would continue to struggle building my career without any family help whatsoever, while they ranked in the big bucks in dealerships my parents had financed for them decades before.

Dad knew I was (finally) ready to be the boss, to run my own studio, without the hundred-mile commute to the city I was making daily. He knew I had no chance of financial success unless I ran my own operation. He was right.

Designing and contracting work for my new studio on my ranch gave me a reason to live after the loss of my Dad.

With few exceptions (only my two younger brothers), none of my five brothers expressed any interest in my ranch or studio. They were city boys and had no interest in the country life, or in me which they made perfectly clear. My Father and Mother held onto the deeds to all their properties including all my brother's car dealerships, homes on the lake and ocean as well as my ranch. There was nothing sinister here. In Dad's eyes, it was smart business and common with men of his generation.

Every asset my parents owned was recorded in their "Black Books" as told to me by both of my parents. Once "in-laws" entered into the equation specific steps were taken to secure the family assets in the event of probable divorces. It was Dad's way to secure his fortune. Unlike my brothers—no business arrangement ever existed between my parents and I. I was never asked to pay them rent. No rental or lease agreement ever existed. My situation was different. The investment in my ranch could never be compared to the multi-millions of dollars my folks spent to set my brothers up in business.

Despite the disparity in our financial investments, my brothers resented our parent's interest in helping me at all. I'll never know why.

Time would reveal the extent my siblings were willing to go to annihilate me.

17

THE CORRUPTION ESCALATES

After Dad's death his attorney continued to "represent" my Mother, whom he had never met or even spoke with—funny, this attorney had plenty of time to cash her checks.

This same attorney began representing my youngest brother's (#5) legal matters in an obvious conflict of interest. My brother had been hand-picked by Dad as executor and was ethically bound to now protect Mom's interests since everything in Dad's estate went to Mom.

The ONLY link my Father's attorney had to his client (Mom) was through my youngest brother. This attorney decided to align himself with the one person he believed could control all the other family members, including his Mother. He was the poster boy for reprehensible solicitors. Without Mom's knowledge or permission he set up a limited liability company transferring Mom's assets, including property, into this company then named my brother "General Manager". The purpose of which was to take control of my Mother's properties from her and transfer control to my brother (#5). This lawyer knew all the legal tricks to play to gain control of an already fractured family in mourning. To him, this was just the price of doing business. No one was to take it personally, but I did. So did Mom.

Not long after Mom challenged her youngest son's authority, I received a package at my ranch. My brother had billed me over $170,000 for my new studio. In a calculating, condescending move, he included a payment book and self-addressed stamped envelopes addressed to him. His letter stated that he expected prompt payment to repay the family trust for the cost of the studio. Though it was Mom's money that built my studio, #5 was now siding with my other brothers who had always opposed my getting a studio in the first place. This was not just a bill for what I knew was a gift from my Father; this was a declaration of war between my brothers and me.

What triggered such vindictive, hateful behavior?
What the hell did I ever do to deserve such animosity?

Once I dismissed my employees and canceled our photoshoot for the day, I called Mom. Through uncontrollable tears, I was able to get the gist of the story across to her. I told Mom I couldn't afford to pay the bill her son had sent me and that I was going to move. Though it took a lot to rile Mom, she hit the roof. She was as mad as I've ever heard her. "Dad and I bought you that ranch and that studio was Dad's gift to you, Susan, his dying wish. You don't owe us one dime for it. Who the hell does your brother think he is? Dad and I gave the boys millions!"

Mom told me not to worry, that she had some calls to make, that she would handle the situation. But I did worry. Dad was gone. Mom was doing her best to handle the estate. The Black Books were missing—no, stolen, and now we discovered her youngest son had turned into a criminal we did not recognize. What was happening here?

When Mom called me back she was still feeling her "Irish." She had called my brother but could not reach him. Typical. She then called Dad's estate planner, whom she had once met at his office across the country. Mom hated the estate planner and let everyone know it, including Dad when he was alive. To Mom, he was a sarcastic up-and-comer who had limited people skills, especially when dealing with women. I understood Mom's reticence to trust him. He gave off signals of gender bias without even opening his mouth.

Still fuming, Mom asked point-blank, "Whose money built Susan's studio?" He answered, "Yours." "Then who the hell told my son to send a bill for $170,000 to Susan?" Mom demanded. Silence. "That's what I thought. Don't ever do this to my daughter again!"

When Mom finally did reach my brother she ordered him to fire both the estate planner AND, Dad's attorney. MY BROTHER REFUSED. This act of recalcitrance created a lance to Mom's heart which would never heal. She never trusted my brother again.

The Good Ole Boy's Club were not use to sharing information, or documents, or property, or control, or millions of dollars with women.

They didn't give a damn which of the five sons happened to be in control of my parents' fortune at any given time after Dad's death. It simply didn't matter to them. The more infighting and division among the family members, the more money they made, as months turned into years.

The circus had come to town and they had caught the brass ring, they were enjoying this free ride.

18

HITTING CLOSE TO HOME

One day out of the blue I had a call from the president of my local bank, she said, "Can you come immediately to the bank? There's something of great importance I must discuss with you."

"Of course," I answered. "I'll be right there.

As I walked into the bank I wondered what the problem was. I had been a customer for fifteen years and never even bounced a check. I had no loans and owed no money. What could it be?

She ushered me into her office and closed the door behind us. I felt like a high school student sent to the principal's office.

Nervous, I asked, "What's up?"

"The FBI has been contacted and I have been ordered to freeze all your bank accounts?"

"What! Why?" I began to cry even though I had no clue what this surreal experience was all about.

"Your brother is involved in a check-kiting ring. The scheme involves three banks, two out of state and this one."

"What are you trying to say? I don't know what that term means."

"Kiting is an attempt to use a bad check to get money or credit. Your brother (#5) has told the authorities that you have no knowledge of the illegal activities, but you helped set up the account here, right?"

"Yes," I said. "We set up the account here when my Mother bought part of the ranch.

"Well, after that deal finished your brother wrote a hot check in the amount of $450,000 on this bank. A small rural bank like ours cannot survive such a catastrophic loss. If the money is not returned immediately, our bank will close."

"What am I going to do? I don't have that kind of money. How could this happen to me?"

When she said nothing I said, "I know your husband is the editor of the local paper. Can we keep this out of the press? I'd like to keep this private. Try to protect my Mom."

"Sure," she said. "I cannot imagine any brother who would do this to his sister."

"He was my favorite brother. I adored him. I don't know what has happened to him."

She gave me a look of pity and hugged me as I left her office. I was afraid to speak to anyone. I was nearly paralyzed with fear.

It was two days before Christmas, a year after Dad died. Once again I would be deliberately excluded from family celebrations of the holidays even though two of my brothers lived close by.

I didn't care about the holidays. I became preoccupied with finding a solution, some way to get that huge amount of money to save my bank and try to keep my brother from being indicted for a federal crime.

The following day, Christmas Eve, I was forced to call Mom and tell her the agonizing news. We both cried and Mom sent a check to the bank.

The next day, Christmas, my sister, feeling no pain, called to scream at me for ruining everyone's Christmas. Somehow in her "pickled" mind, I alone was responsible for ruining everyone's Christmas. I could barely breathe from the recent events. That night I attended Christmas Mass alone, returned home to no holiday tree of gifts. I put a TV dinner in the oven, ate my cardboard feast, curled up under my electric blanket and cried myself to sleep.

At this point, Mom and I couldn't separate the good guys from the bad guys because to us they were ALL bad guys.

19

MOM'S FARM UP NORTH

For a couple of years after Dad's death, Mom returned in the summer to their farm on the lake up North. Though my siblings and their families visited her there, she was lonely. She decided to sell the farm. It was too big, too much work, and held too many painful memories of Dad.

One day Mom called and said, "Everyone is coming to take what they want. I am cleaning out the farm. Can you come?"

"Not right now, Mom. I'm in the middle of a photoshoot for my big account. But I'll come as soon as I can."

"You better hurry, Susie. The other kids are cleaning me out."

Mom said this jokingly but there was an undertone of fear in her voice. "Well, will you save a couple of things for me?" I asked.

"Sure. What would you like?"

"The Tiffany-style light fixture in the dining room and Dad's concrete Blessed Mother statue that's in the yard."

"That's all? The boys rented moving trucks and they've been hauling away bedroom sets, dining room suites, tractors, boats, and everything that's not nailed down."

"Thanks, Mom. I'll be happy with those two items."

"I'll be there soon," I promised.

Getting away was difficult for me because I ran my 1,000-acre ranch. I was responsible for cattle, horses, sheep as well as dogs and cats. Friends called me "Ellie Mae Clampett" because of my affinity for my land and my animals. I also ran my studio and art directed the photoshoots for my multi-million dollar account. Clients and employees depended on me, as well as my critters.

When I finally arranged enough time off for a visit to see Mom at our farm, I was shocked upon my arrival. Ninety-five percent of my parents' things were gone. It felt like the only thing my siblings had left for me were the dead flies on the windowsill. Mom had secured the Tiffany fixture and the Blessed Mother statue. "I tried to tell you," Mom said. "Your brother (#2) is coming back to help me close up and put the property on the market in a few days." It was painful to leave Mom. I knew she was fragile and vulnerable. As I left to drive back home with the few items Mom gave me, I cried for the first hundred miles. It broke my heart to leave her behind.

I got a call after arriving home that something went wrong during the time my brother visited Mom. Somehow Mom's house at the farm caught fire. Whether it was an unattended candle or a cigarette igniting after an ashtray had been emptied in a bag of trash, no one knew. Or, no one was saying. Mom blamed her son and my brother blamed her. When I talked to Mom, she explained that the fire was confined to the kitchen but caused quite a bit of damage. "Was anyone hurt?" I asked.

"Thankfully, no. I don't mind telling you Susie, but I'm scared. You know how it is with your hothead brother, I have to walk around on eggshells. I'm afraid to say anything or do anything. I'm still so mad at him for his dealership scandal and what he did to Dad. I love him and he's my son, but I did not start that fire."

This incident started a rift between Mom and my brother, which was to last for two long years, during which time neither one spoke to the other.

Unfortunately, this wasn't the last fire to involve this brother and my Mother, at one of her other homes.

20

"THE PRODIGAL" SKULKING IN THE SHADOWS

The last holiday season Mom was alive after her eldest son showed up drunk and tried to embezzle hundreds of thousands of dollars from her, the stage had been set, the door opened, for the son she called "the prodigal," (#2) a.k.a. "the hothead."

After a fall-out with Mom, this son had not spoken to her for two years which hurt her deeply. As was typical of my brothers, their dominance for power never abated. When one son retreated another would charge forward in his bid to take control of Mom (and her fortune). Although Mom never forgot the abuse, she welcomed the abuser(s) with open arms. These were her children.

By New Years, after son #1 had left, son #2 moved into Mom's house. He never announced or asked permission to move in—he just did it.

He took over our late Father's office and proceeded to set up files for every asset he could find. He took over all Mom's bank accounts, her safe deposit boxes, all her jewelry, as well as her home safe. He then hired a local attorney and accountant he told Mom would represent HER interests.

Mom was smarter than that. The prodigal son was heavily in debt to Mom. This was the son who lost his dealership, dealer license and nearly his freedom in his fraud and racketeering trial.

This was also the son, (along with his #3 brother) who stole the Black Books the day Dad died. My brother (#2) announced that #3 would be paying Mom's new attorney and CPA.

Mom was furious her son had taken over not just her fortune but also her home. I witnessed Mom telling him she did not trust ANY lawyer chosen by any of her sons—that because they were hired and paid by her sons his loyalty would be to them—NOT her!

Mom was right, but my bully of a brother didn't care. He was running the show now and he didn't care what anybody else thought, least of all his Mother.

In short time brothers #1 and #4 would align themselves with the bully (#2), as well as my sister to join an unhealthy partnership controlled by the most notorious brother of all, #3.

Once in control their strategy was to achieve three goals:
  1. To steal as much of Mom's estate as possible for themselves and their wives and ex-wives
  2. To expose Dad's "hand-picked" favorite son, (#5) for his criminal behavior and to recover any remaining assets he controlled and
  3. To destroy Susan. Financially as well as emotionally, and to ensure her total and complete ostracism from the family.

As incredulous as this sounds my siblings all shared the same condition; Alcoholism. It was the unifying factor in their unholy alliance to inflict as much pain as possible to the one kid who wasn't a drunk—me. Mom asked me to accompany her when my brother took her to the attorney "chosen and paid' by my brothers. The meeting was an ambush intended to put me on notice that I would be forced to justify my existence at my ranch and studio when the time came.

I was drilled by this attorney whom I had never met, about where I lived and did I pay my parents rent to live there? (Prompted by my brother). When I answered, "No," my brother's attorney snapped, "Don't you think you should!"

I sat shocked and mute. This was a setup. My brothers had already planned to go after the one asset my parents had bought for me, my ranch.

My brother just sat there while a total stranger insulted his sister after he had squandered millions of my parents' money over his criminal history.

By now four of my parent's car dealerships had gone bankrupt with a fifth on life support. My brothers had squandered their opportunities for success and security. In the process, they had destroyed my Father's good name and reputation. I saw the handwriting on the wall, so did Mom.

Stealing from Mom was as easy as shooting ducks in a barrel. Stealing from Susan became a blood sport. They were already sharpening their knives.

The last time #2 spoke to me was the last time I saw my Mother alive at her home in Florida. Mom had asked me to come down and help her inventory her things. "The hothead" called me into my late Dad's office and his nostrils were flaring like that of an Arabian horse. He was mad. More than mad, he was fuming.

"Listen, Susan, I don't give a shit about Mom's jewelry or personal things. Everybody knows that Mom wants you girls (my sister and I) to get that stuff."

Shaking in barely controlled violence he showed me proof that our youngest brother had stolen millions of dollars from Mom's estate. I wanted to say, "I already know," but I didn't dare say a word. I could have quipped, "So have you," but I would have come out on the short end of that altercation.

He pointed his finger at me from across Dad's desk and said, "I never stole a f-ing dime, not a f-ing dime from Dad, but he stole from my brother and me. You better know that Dad was a thief and a liar."

I stood there dumbfounded. I wanted to say, "Dad's dead. Why spill your guts to me? What do I have to do with your unresolved issues about Dad? What can I do about this? Nothing. Not one thing." Instead, I stayed silent. I didn't need to defend Dad. His life spoke for itself. I knew his legacy as if it were written in stone. Nothing anyone said was going to change the truth about Dad. I wasn't going to argue with my brother. I could see the pain behind his anger. The truth I knew about Dad was NOT what his corrupt sons believed.

I was beginning to finally put the pieces of the puzzle together—why my family despised me for so long without cause: First, I wasn't an alcoholic as they were, and Second, I reminded them too much of Dad. Dad had always been my hero, my role model in life. I didn't have to look far for verification of my Dad's character.

There's an old saying 'you can judge a man by the company he keeps.' I knew the people Dad surrounded himself with. They were all self-made men from the 'Greatest Generation.' The company Dad kept were role models—men rooted in faith and proven in adversity.

That was good enough for me.

I was perceptive enough to understand my brothers' twisted thinking. Whenever my parents bailed them out of trouble, legal or otherwise, Dad considered it a loan, but they considered it a gift. They had no intention of repaying our folks for what they believed was an entitlement.

In their minds, Dad was stealing from them. Tossing their own Mother aside and taking control of her home, her assets, and her millions was their way of retribution, of taking back something that was owed to them.

They couldn't have been more wrong, or more selfish.

21

ROCKING THE BOAT

My brothers were masters at manipulation either by lying to get what they wanted or outright stealing. They certainly were not restrained by the Ten Commandments which they thought of as only "10 suggestions," nor by the Rule of Law, which was why they kept their attorneys' on speed dial.

Mom knew her sons had no skills for resolving conflicts so, to her, the trick was to have no conflicts. Walk on eggshells, do whatever you must, but don't tick off the boys.

I had trouble trying to run my business with deadlines, and employees, in addition to managing my ranch duties. I felt powerless to help Mom deal with the weekly barrage of problems my brothers inflicted on her after Dad's death since I lived across the country.

In one upsetting call, Mom got wind that her sons (and their wives) had plans to turn Mom's home into a bed and breakfast when she died. She blew her stack and told everyone who would listen, she wanted her home sold after her death and the money divided among her own children. She feared her gold-digging daughter-in-law would move in when she already had her own mansion. As if this revelation wasn't upsetting enough, three of my brothers (#2, 3 and 4) showed up unannounced for a vacation at Mom's.

"Susan, You'll never believe what those bastards did!"

"Which bastards?" I asked though I knew good and well whom she meant.

Your brothers (2,3, & 4) were here for a week. They took $111,000 of my money—MY MONEY—and bought a boat! They named it after me and made me go with them for a ride. It's huge with an upstairs and a downstairs. They told me the thing is seaworthy, that it is made for big ocean excursions. They said they bought it for me. Me? That's a lie. They bought it for themselves. THEY'RE SPENDING ALL MY MONEY, SUSAN, AND I'M NOT EVEN DEAD YET. I hate boats. You know that. I'm almost eighty years old. What the hell do I want with a damn boat?"

Mom was on a roll, so I did not interrupt.

"Susie, I'm physically sick. I've been vomiting ever since they left. They made me sit downstairs with #4 while the big shots (sons #2 and 3) drove the boat. It made me ill. I'm so upset. I have no idea what to do. So I called you."

Mom paused to take a deep breath.

"Do you want me to fly down and be with you?"

"No, I can't ask you to do that. I'll call my friend to come be with me. She said to call if I ever needed help."

"Are you okay right now?"

"I think so. I LOCKED MYSELF IN MY ROOM. I don't know when the boys might return. I don't want to see them, Susan. I don't want to face them."

"I understand. I'm just so sorry. I feel heartsick and helpless. I —

"It's alright. I'll figure out something. Thanks for listening. It helps me. It really does. I don't have anyone else to talk to."

After Mom hung up I wondered what kind of a boat you could buy for $111,000. It would get you one heck of a nice car. I never saw the boat. My brothers kept its location a secret. But they were slipping, getting ridiculous. Did they think they could get away with passing off a downsized version of the Queen Mary as a gift for my aging Mother? A gift bought with her money? Mom knew exactly what was happening to her money. But she was nearly powerless at this point to do anything to stop the bleeding.

Increasingly it did not matter what Mom wanted. Dad was gone and my brothers now saw my parents' estate as their own. Mom was only a temporary obstacle to them.

I was learning one of the most painful lessons of my life, that in most disputes involving a will (or trust) the executor begins to think it's THEIR money. Their estate, their jackpot.

"Hangers on" will attach themselves, like barnacles on a boat, to see how far they can go to grab their share of the pot.

It broke my heart to see Mom living in fear of her own children, having to "lock" herself in her bedroom to escape their unannounced visits.

Nearing eighty, Mom was a very private person. She refused live-in help and became increasingly isolated because she found it too embarrassing to divulge anything about her disgraceful sons.

At this point, my biggest fear was losing Mom, whom I adored. Little did I know my biggest fear was just around the corner.

22

MOM'S DEATH

After my brother moved into my Mother's home—uninvited—Mom began to feel unsafe, not from intruders, but from her son. Against her wishes he had taken control of her whole world and she resented it. My brother (#2) would often show up at all hours of the day or night with "friends" including his ex-wife whom Mom despised.

The only place Mom felt safe was in her bedroom. Since my brother had keys to everything she owned (including her bedroom doors). Mom began tying pantyhose around the inside double door handles to prevent anyone from invading her privacy. My brothers, as well as their wives, stole items Mom cherished including his awards and war metals along with Dad's American flag in its display case, which draped his coffin. With each visit came more missing items.

When Mom told me about her pantyhose security system I got upset and told her so. My fear was her inability to escape should there be an emergency. I blamed my brothers and their wives for stealing Mom's sense of security, beyond her possessions. My Mother's house had an alarm system which she used every day. It was the intruders WITHIN her own family she feared the most. With good reason.

The last time Mom and I talked we chatted and laughed for two hours. I had made plans to fly down to see her within days, and she told me she couldn't wait. As we said our goodbyes I told Mom I loved her to which she answered, "I love you too, Susie. More than you'll ever know."

That was the last time I ever heard my Mother's beautiful voice.

The next day my sister called me at work and blurted out, "MOM'S DEAD, and her dog too."

My knees buckled. The shock left me breathless. I began to cry. How? When? Why?

My brother (#2) discovered Mom, who had been killed in a fire in her home. He had called his "comrades" (#3 & #4) but refused to call Mom's other four children. My sister found out from a paramedic friend (near Mom's town) who was called when the fire call came through. I made immediate plans to fly down to Mom's. When my brothers heard this I was ordered NOT to come because Mom's house was considered a possible crime scene and was cordoned off until an investigation had taken place.

Later I was to discover this was a lie my brothers told to allow my brother's (#3) wife to fly down to have the locks changed so that my brothers and their wives could access Mom's home to help themselves to anything they wanted. As my Mother's daughter, I was never again allowed to access my Mother's home.

My brother's wife removed Mom's address books making it impossible for me to contact Mom and Dad's lifelong friends about her death. My brother's wife, who had not spoken to me for twenty years, called to tell me the fire had destroyed all of Mom's clothes. This is the woman who commandeered my own Mother's home at the insistence of her husband, had the locks changed so I would never be permitted inside again. My Mother despised this woman.

She had invaded the sanctity of my Mother's home and was given "permission" by her husband (brother #3) to plan my Mother's funeral. The truth was Mom's clothes NEVER burned in the fire which took her life. Mom died of smoke inhalation confined to one room only in her home. Her bedroom. When the fire started she had been asleep. She woke in a panic and tried to save her small dog. In her horror, she was unable to remove the pantyhose securing her bedroom doors. Mom was overcome trying to save her beloved doggie's life.

They died together.

Mom's home, which Dad designed and built, was 11,000 sq. feet. Mom's wardrobe was extensive and stored in cedar-lined closets throughout three stories. My Mother was fastidious about her closets for two reasons: first, cedar-lined closets protected her clothes from the damp ocean air, and second, her closets were carpeted and off-limits to her dog. Mom was religious about always keeping all her closets doors closed. The fire never reached her closets. Her clothes had survived the fire.

Funny, how Mom's full-length mink and sable coats survived, but nothing else. My brother's (#3) estranged wife had a history of lying. This was just another example.

I bought the dress Mom was buried in.

Years later, my brother's wife lied that I, Susan, "did not care enough" about my Mother to immediately fly down when she was killed. Witnesses will corroborate that I had reservations to fly to Mom's within an hour of hearing about my Mother's tragic death. For this woman to question my intent and devotion to my Mother is beyond cruel. To this day I hate this woman with every fiber of my being.

My Mother would have hated this woman's invasion of her home, especially at the expense of her own daughter's rightful place as the one person chosen to carry out her funeral wishes.

Outside I held my temper as I prepared to bury my beloved Mother. Inside I felt violated and disrespected. I wasn't sure how I would make it through the difficult days ahead.

*****

It was my brothers' decision to plan Mom's funeral for June 27th, my birthday. I was never consulted. Their choice of dates was deliberately intended to hurt me, my birthday would never be the same.

My only goal, other than surviving that day, was making sure my Mother's little dog was placed in the coffin and buried with her. I made that happen.

Not one of my five brothers or their wives offered one word of comfort to me in front of our Mother's coffin. I hugged each one of them, looked them straight in the eyes and said, "I am so sorry for your loss and I love you."

Not one of them said a word to me.

Not a word.

My aunt, Mom's sister, cried when she witnessed how I was treated. People saw for themselves how vicious my brothers had become, how downright cruel.

As the procession into the church began for Mom's funeral Mass, my sister whispered to me she thought our brothers had "something to do with Mom's death." That left me shaking. As planned, not one of my family members would sit with me in the pew.

I had to stay strong and focus on delivering my Mother's eulogy, which she had asked me to do after Dad's funeral.

I was in a church surrounded by people who hated me. I hated public speaking, it scared me to death—but I was determined to tell the world how much I appreciated and loved my Mother.

During Mom's service, the Bishop spoke directly to the disunity in my family. He called for unity. He took the opportunity of my Mother's funeral to berate her children, which I thought was inappropriate at the time. (I consider it MORE inappropriate today).

I knew that my Dad must have shared his frustrations with his friend the Bishop. Obviously the Bishop knew the problems the boys had caused my parents. Nevertheless, not ALL of my Mother's children were thieves and the opportunity to chastise the entire clan was, I believe, in very poor taste. For the record, this Bishop had never met me.

As the Mass began I focused on the floral arrangements I had ordered for Mom's casket, as well as the church. My brother's wife had given strict orders to the florist to get her "approval" for all funeral arrangements. I had to read the florist the riot act when he attempted to tell me any flowers I was ordering for my OWN Mother would need to be approved by my brother's estranged wife. "Approved" was his word. He got the message when he realized I was gunning for bear and would raise holy hell if he didn't respect my wishes and position as Daughter. Once I reminded him whose Mother was lying in the coffin, he acquiesced.

As the only designer in the family, I was not about to be sidelined by anyone when it came to flowers. The biggest arrangements on the altar matched the spray on Mom's coffin. I knew her favorite flowers and made certain they were incorporated.

Not forgetting her little doggy I designed a bed of dark green leaves with baby's breath upon which was the outline of a big dog bone of yellow bottom mums.

As the ceremony proceeded, the Bishop paused. He told the congregation that one of my Mother's children had prepared a eulogy. My sister had told me that our eldest brother had prepared some words to say. I did not want to upstage him. So I waited. I was surprised when my brother did not stand up. He did not move. Finally, I thought, somebody needs to stand up, so I did. After lovingly stroking Mom's coffin, I walked up the stairs to the altar podium. When I turned around I was glad I had on my tortoiseshell reading glasses, the ones my sister always said made me look like 'Murphy Brown." My glasses blurred the faces of the congregation, so I never knew who sat where in the church. I was glad I could only see the coffin immediately in front of me. I felt amazingly confident and calm. I had a mission to accomplish. I was on stage and ready to deliver the most important speech of my life, my tribute to my Mother.

These are the exact words of my eulogy:

Dearest Mom,

Words cannot begin to express the depth of our heartbreak in losing you. We all know how very difficult life was for you after losing Dad and we knew you longed to be with him. Well, now you are.

We are comforted to know you are now in the loving arms of Jesus, with Our Blessed Mother; Mary, nearby. We will find solace in the future to think of you by Dad's side in the company of Grandmom and Grandpop, Uncle ____dear Aunt ____ and just days ago beautiful ____.

In the Bible, in St. John, Chapter 14, it says, "In my Father's house there are many dwelling places. If it were not so, I would have told you for I am going away. To prepare a place for you—and when I go and make ready a place for you, I will come back again and will take you to myself so that where I am, you may be also."

Mom, your new white house is finally finished! It took Dad six-and-a-half years to build this one and Jesus was his carpenter. I can't imagine how big that house is going to be! But I am happy that it will be yours and Dad's for all eternity.

Mom, Dad always treated you like a "Princess." He gave you everything money could buy, except one thing: a crown. So it was no surprise when you named your puppy "Princess." No one values the unconditional love of a pet more than I. Princess was your best little buddy. She was always by your side with her green bunny toy. Even in the end, she was there. Now she's by your side for all eternity. (I hope puppies are potty trained in heaven.)

Mom, you were beautiful and elegant and funny and so very fragile. After Dad died you told me, you finally understood the lonely walk of a single woman—and it drew us closer. Thank you for giving me life and for a lifetime of memories I will always cherish.

Mom, Dad gave you everything he could but he couldn't give you a crown because even Dad knew it wasn't his place to do that. Dad knew you had to earn your crown in this life, all by yourself. Well, now you have.

Yesterday when I kissed you good-bye for the last time on my birthday I gave you a crown. Now you've earned your crown down here, more importantly, now you've earned your crown up there in heaven and Princess earned hers too. (In heaven the diamonds are real!)

Mom, help us to earn our own crowns. We all need your help.

Mom, your life was one incredible journey. From a humble beginning, Dad and you built an incredible life together. You traveled the world together meeting movie stars, Presidents and even a Pope. And yet, you were happiest with the simple pleasures life could afford: your game shows, calls from your children, your puppy.

We are all grateful for having had you in our lives. We will carry with us forever the best parts of who you are and what you stood for—elegance, beauty, courage and always forgiveness.

Thank you for the wisdom in those last private words you said to me the last time we were together. They validated my entire existence.

Mom, we miss and love you forever. Give Dad our love. Thank you for everything.

Love forever,
Susan

*****

Years later my sister told me they all hated me for my eulogies of Dad and Mom. I reminded her there was no rulebook for eulogies, that anyone could give one. They all had their chance and they blew it. I had my chance, and I took it. Those two eulogies I wrote by myself, were the proudest moments of my life.

23

THE NIGHTMARE BEGINS

At the small reception my brothers had arranged after Mom's funeral at a local bar, my siblings hit the bar with the same intensity that the Allies had hit the beaches of Normandy.

After some heavy drinking my brother (#3) feeling no pain, approached me, obviously ruffled by the Bishop's remarks during the service about the disunity within the family.

This brother had not spoken to me in twenty years following his firing me for something so abhorrent no one seemed to know what it was. But there he was, stoned, and frankly scary looking, demanding me to apologize to him for what I had (allegedly) done to him decades before.

I could not apologize for an offense I had no I idea I had committed. He got his desired result by reducing me to tears within minutes of burying Mom. My brother's outburst was outrageous and unprovoked. It proved to me that this man was helpless in exhibiting any self-control even at his own Mother's funeral. My brother was incapable of rational behavior and that frightened me. For the first time, I began to fear what he could do to me. He had an arsenal of guns. My sister's own words walking with me into church, rang in my head.

I remember thinking "if" my brothers DID have something to do with Mom's death, then they would one day answer for that.

I had enough on my mind and it wouldn't bring Mom back, so I let it go.

24

REACHING OUT FOR HELP

When I returned home from my Mother's funeral, I called my Father's CPA, on Madison Avenue in New York. I thought I could trust him because he had worked for my Dad, professed to be a family friend, and had been working with #5 supposedly to help Mom. I told him my fears and concerns. He told me he knew my youngest brother had NOT handled the estate as my Dad instructed. He also concurred that if any or all of my brothers were now in charge of the estate that it would be, in his words, "disastrous… because [my Father] never trusted his four older sons. He asked me to write him with my concerns, which I did.

It would be years before I learned why my calls and letters to him fell on deaf ears. I learned that this man had copied my letters to all my brothers as well their attorneys. He also began working directly for brothers 2 and 3 and participated in the transfer of millions of dollars of Trust properties in the form of favorable "Sweetheart deals" for my brothers. This CPA betrayed his long-standing friendship with my late Father. What he cared about, was the money that bought his loyalty—it didn't matter to him who wrote the checks.

As a result he, had no interest in helping me, and less in carrying out my Father's wishes. My brothers had used intimidation to control each other as well as our Mother. Now they were attempting to control me. I became the lone female voice of opposition; I was the obvious target of the "Good Ole Boys' Club." Controlling power through controlling information became their strategy. Handling my parent's estate was a guy's domain and a guy's game. Heaven help a woman if she started sniffing around the clubhouse.

I was not a woman used to asking anyone for help unless I really needed it. Beyond my legal advisors, I sought help from people who were lifelong friends of my parents. People whose children I once babysat.

I reached out to longtime friends who knew my family history well. People my Dad had helped secure dealer franchises as well as executive positions. Dad's friends were appalled by my brothers' actions yet not one—NOT ONE—was willing to make a call on my behalf.

To this day I am convinced that had even one man—one colleague of my Fathers'— been willing to question my brothers' campaign to remove me from my home and ranch—it would have sent a powerful signal that Susan was not alone. I wonder how they would have reacted had their wife or daughter been in my position?

I never felt more alone in my life. My brothers' strategy of isolation was working. At one point my attorney cautioned me, "You know their trying to get you to commit suicide?" to which I snapped, "Don't you think I know that!?!" At that moment I resented him for even saying that word, for even planting that seed in my brain.

There were more times than I could count where I had prayed God would take me in my sleep.

I wasn't afraid of dying.

I was tired of living.

25

THE FIRST MEETING

Two months after Mom's funeral my attorneys and I tried to obtain information about my Mother's estate and the distribution of assets. We were being stonewalled (not surprisingly) by my brothers and their attorneys, by design, to make my life more difficult.

Dragging legal procedures out over months and years, (often decades), is a common ploy to bleed their opponent financially into submission. This was only one strategy my brothers' lawyer's embraced to try to destroy me.

It did not matter that I was my parents' daughter, an heir, beneficiary to their estate. I was treated like the bastard red-headed stepchild. Even my own attorneys were shocked at how unprofessional and crude the opposition's legal teams were. Professional ethics and courtesies were totally ignored. Phone calls went unanswered, and again and again my advisors complained they had never seen such an estate "nightmare" as my family in all their years of practicing law.

Eventually I was able to get a meeting scheduled with my attorneys and my youngest brother and his attorney (who had also represented Mom).

I had come to despise this lawyer for three reasons: First—he refused to execute my Mom's mandates (who became his client upon Dad's death), Second—while supposedly representing my Mother he was secretly acting as her sons' council in direct opposition to the client who was paying him—my Mother. This was a serious breach of ethics. Third—this same attorney referred to me, (whom he had never met or spoken with) as a "freeloader."

Again, Mom ordered him fired for this remark. Again, my brother refused to do so, exposing my brother's loyalty to the hired help and extreme prejudice against his own Mother and sister.

Once the meeting began my brother appeared visibly upset Mom had died not trusting him as her executor. He admitted to serious financial losses running Mom's dealership. He revealed he "borrowed" 2.5 million dollars from Mom's trust which he intended to repay. He never did.

By the time this meeting had happened, the "brothers" had split into different camps. #2, 3, and 4 were aligned soon to be joined by brother #1 (who always despised #2 and #3) as well as my sister (who always followed #1's wishes).

The "outgoing" executor (#5) was on his own, but still in control of millions in assets.

I was
Alone.
I knew my baby brother would live the rest of his life with the guilt of disappointing Mom and Dad. When I saw him that day—I wasn't about to throw salt on his enormous self-inflicted emotional wounds.

I believed Shakespeare said it best, "Cowards die many times before their deaths; the valiant never taste of death but once."

As the meeting concluded my council's objective was to file a motion with the court to allow me access to Mom's home.

When the subject of my ranch came up, we were promised "the letter" Mom signed (prior to her death) which my brother's attorney held—would be "delivered" to me.

That "letter" was in addition to TWO quick claim deeds / WITH attached legal descriptions, Mom had signed giving me my ranch.

My brother and his attorney made sure I NEVER got Mom's "letter." They also made sure I would never see those deeds.

After the meeting, I drove to the cemetery to see Mom and Dad. I sat on the bench opposite their crypts and sobbed my eyes out.

In my mind, what my siblings and their attorneys had done was unzip their flies and pissed on my parent's graves. Not one of these men was doing what my parents had wished. Not one.

26

SIX MONTHS AFTER MOM'S DEATH

Six months after the funeral my brothers had done nothing to settle Mom's estate or distribute any of her assets (except, of course, to their wives and children).

My lawyers decided we should protest in court the legal swearing of my brother #2 as executor (who had moved into Mom's home—uninvited) and his (joined at the hip) brother #3. Legally a judge must swear in an executor/or trustee to handle an estate, I was told.

I testified in front of the judge I believed my brothers to be irresponsible alcoholics incapable of administering our Mother's estate properly. My efforts, despite being called a "very powerful witness" failed. My brothers were sworn in as executors replacing my youngest brother legally in that position. The court did slap a two million dollar bond on each brother for anything they might TRY to steal from the estate. Little did this impotent judge realize the stealing had been going on for decades despite his (bond) deterrent.

Who was going to "police" my brothers? The courts—hardly.

I avoided eye contact with my brothers but my attorney commented how bad my brother (#2)—the executor, looked in court.

The only satisfaction I came away with that day was that I had had the guts to get up in court and call my brothers "Alcoholics" for the record, to their faces. Something my parents never did.

At the time my brother (#2) was sworn in by the court, he had already learned he was dying of cancer.

Serious health issues were grounds for a judge to refuse to swear in an executor. My brother's attorney was unwilling to share that fact with the court.

Within months my brother would be unable to fulfill his duties as executor and turn his job over to the most diabolical brother of all: # 3. The ship had hit the iceberg, now it was only a matter of time.

27

REVISITING MOM'S MANSION

Months after Mom's death I was still denied access to my Mother's home. My attorney filed a motion with the court, in her state to allow me to enter the house. Despite being a legal heir to her estate my brothers' (#2 and 3) attorney maintained I had NO right to enter.

Knowing he would lose in court their attorney suddenly "allowed" me to enter Mom's home, but I was absolutely forbidden to take anything." This attorney never denied access to my brother's wives who removed dozens of items belonging to my Mother, including all her jewelry, antiques as well as expensive perfumes from Paris.

As the moment arrived for me to gain access I was told it was to be under the supervision of a "guard" from my brothers' attorneys' office. This Brunhilda was a big, homely, butch-looking woman straight out of Disney's central casting. She reproached me for arriving early and entering Mom's home before she could search me. I was then informed I had only one hour allotted time in the house. No one had informed me of those ground rules—which I NEVER would have accepted.

I told the bitch to go screw herself, that I would leave my Mother's home when I was damn good and ready and not one minute sooner.

She recoiled with, "How dare you question my authority. Don't you know who my boss is? Don't you know who he is representing?

I answered, "I DO know, and I don't give a shit!" What were they going to do, call the police and arrest me in my own Mother's home I owned 1/7 of?

I was gunning for bear and she knew it. She hid in a bathroom to call her boss.

As I walked towards my Mother's bedroom I got choked up. I was about to see the spot where she died. Suddenly two electricians startled me, "Pardon me, Miss, but we have work to complete, can you kindly step aside?"

"No, I will NOT step aside."

After a screaming match the workmen left. I had been promised privacy to mourn in my Mother's bedroom. I even had to fight for that.

My next task was to go downstairs to see what was left of Mom's personal possessions. Since we had inventoried everything in January, I knew everything she owned. My first thought when I opened the door: "Mom would be horrified." My second thought: "Where is the rest of it?" Everything my Mother had owned (except for her jewelry which had already been confiscated by my brothers' wife), was tossed into one big room. It looked like a junky, disorganized garage sale. Waterford crystal was thrown in with Tupperware. Expensive European clocks were lying on the floor. Mom's sterling silver was stacked next to a stuffed doll. My artwork leaned against a wobbly card table. I remembered the horse trailer with the out-of-state tags that had been parked in Mom's driveway after her funeral. I made a mental note of everything that was missing, then, I photographed everything that was left. And I mean EVERYTHING.

My attorney had asked me to do this as a means of comparing the inventory Mom and I had done to the (grossly incomplete) inventory "the executors" would eventually file with the court.

As I turned to leave my Mother's home forever, my shoe caught the edge of something pink. It was one of Mom's powder puffs with her trademark fuchsia rouge. As I picked it up, I could not contain my tears. That small round powder puff had touched my Mother's cheek. I slipped it into my pocket and walked out. I could now prove my brothers, and their wives, had stolen thousands of dollars in furnishings and personal belongings. I dared them to prosecute me for stealing a power puff. I was never allowed to set foot in my Mother's home again.

After suffering decades of abuse at the hands of my brothers, I doubt if one jury in the world would have convicted me had I strangled that Brunhilda for disrespecting my moment to mourn my Mother at the very spot where she met her Maker.

For the record, none of the hundreds of items my brothers and their wives stole from my Mother's home were ever recovered or returned. My attorneys never filed a report with the court for those stolen items. It just wasn't a priority to them. They didn't care, but I did. And so would Mom!

28

"MERRY CHRISTMAS, SUSAN"

Four days before Christmas, I received a letter from my brother's attorney at my ranch. I knew this was unethical because, legally, once I was represented by counsel, I was NOT to be contacted by any legal representatives except through my attorneys.

Since when did playing by the rules matter to these bottom feeders?

My brother's attorney "assumed" that since he could find no lease or written agreement allowing me permission to reside on the property (my ranch), I had no legal right to be there.

This narrow-minded lawyer assumed my arrangement with my parents to be a "business" transaction. It never was.

They knew Mom had signed two deeds giving me legal ownership of the ranch. They also knew those documents though "promised" were never delivered to me, against Mom's orders.

They were putting me on notice that I would be forced to fight the biggest legal battle of all—for my ranch.

When my attorney asked my brother why he ordered the "eviction" letter in late December, he answered, "Because we wanted to ruin Susan's Christmas."

He got his Christmas wish.

29

THE ULTIMATE INSULT

In an attempt to protect me from losing my ranch my attorney filed a "quiet title" action which was signed by the judge. This was a default judgment since my brothers and their lawyers failed to appear in court. All we had to do was wait the required six-month appeal period.

Just six days before the deadline to appeal, my attorney gave me the devastating news: my brothers had filed in time to overturn the quiet title action.

By the time another year had passed, we returned to court, the judge ruled in favor of my brothers. I lost my ranch.

Details of the court proceedings only became available long after the decision came down. I was prohibited from witnessing the proceedings for EIGHT (8) hours and only allowed to testify for a total of five (5) minutes. I was called into the courtroom at 3:10 p.m. and was dismissed at 3:15 p.m.

How was it possible that this judge would not allow me, 1. In the courtroom to determine the fate of my ranch and, 2. To prevent me from testifying on my own behalf for more than a five minute period? I was never allowed to be cross examined by my own attorney.

The exact court recording quoted the judge's reasoning for overturning his original ruling. He said, "It's a big piece of land, and there are a lot of kids, so I'm overturning my original ruling."

Court records disclosed that the attorney, working for my youngest brother, the man who called me a "freeloader" testified that his "client" (Mom, now dead) had requested that he prepare not one, but TWO warranty deeds to my ranch, but NOT to execute, record, or deliver them to Susan.

That was a damn lie!

My Mother was not a stupid woman. She would NEVER have instructed a lawyer she never met—never even spoke to on the phone—to prepare two deeds to protect her daughter from ever losing her home—then order him NOT to do anything with them.

Why did he prepare two deeds? Who has two deeds to their home? (Nobody

I know)

Without ever speaking with my Mother—how did he know what she wanted for her daughter?

He also testified Susan and her Mother had a fight and Mom wanted me thrown off of the ranch.

Sorry for my language: That was a God-damned lie.

There was never a fight. My Mother never changed her mind to deed me my ranch. I will submit to any lie detector as long as this attorney does as well, and BOTH results are made public.

Name the place and time. I dare you!

*****

It doesn't take much of a man to pervert the truth about a Mother and daughter whose property and good names were damaged as a result of his spurious lies.

I promise you this: come Judgment Day when this guy stands before the heavenly gates, I know of one Mother who'll be standing by with her thumbs down.

What goes around.

30

JUSTICE FOR ALL?

As weeks turned into months, and months turned into years, the legal proceedings continued. In a concerted attempt to drain me financially—any and all attempts for rational, reasonable resolutions were rejected. I was learning, the hard way, how the legal system worked. It worked for the rich and powerful, not for the working man or woman. The procedures, the legalese language used in legal documents is incomprehensible to most of us. I was naïve. I believed in the Rule of Law. In telling the truth, and in following the rules. That was, and is, who I am.

The "legal" system I was now exposed to ignored the laws, bent the rules, and lied under oath in court as well as in depositions. No one held them accountable. No one gave a damn about the truth.

I saw no respect for a woman alone, grieving the loss of not only the parents she adored, but the family she helped them raise.

I believe that judge who wouldn't allow me to testify for more than five (5) minutes (to save me from losing my home) had already made his decision long before the hearing.

He deliberately kept me from testifying—he didn't want to hear the truth. This wasn't about "Susan." This was about a woman who he was told had no legal claim to a "big piece of land." My attorneys believed I was too credible a witness (if allowed to testify) who would have made his decision much more difficult.

I was denied that opportunity.

In the end—revenge was their form of justice.

I'll bet you a steak dinner that not one of the many letters I wrote, (which were stolen from my Mother's home) about my intention to SHARE my ranch with my siblings and their families, was ever introduced into evidence in court. Not one.

Everyone who worked for or knew my brothers and sister just assumed I was as selfish as they were and would never share my ranch.

Nothing in my past remotely suggested I had a history of selfish behavior.

Nothing.

What an insult to my character.

31

PREPARING FOR TRIAL BY DEPOSITION

Four years after Mom's funeral there was no resolution to settle her estate—by design. The only weapon I had was the protracted legal system to force decisions to be made which should have been resolved years earlier.

Since my brothers were already living off of Mom's money, they weren't inconvenienced in the least.

After the hearing which overturned my right to my ranch, my attorney filed a lawsuit against my brothers to recover the rightful ownership of my ranch. As it was explained to me I would have to prove in court that it was my Mother's "intent" to give me the ranch. It was that simple. Proving Mom's intent was akin to proving the Pope was Catholic.

Crowded court dockets pushed the trial date well into the next year. Depositions were scheduled across the country in preparation for trial. Neither of my attorneys adequately prepared me for the experience of being deposed for five hours. Beyond the purpose of attaining information, my deposition was intended to be a forum whereby my brothers' legal team had decided to harass, insult, and intimidate me. It became clear that I had been investigated in what was a witch hunt intended to embarrass or even blackmail me in the future. They found nothing even remotely malevolent in my past, I am sure to their disappointment.

They asked about one "cowboy" I was attracted to who was married. I knew immediately which brother had volunteered this information since I had never shared that private fact with another human being. (It was brother #4) And, for the record, I never had an affair or even an inappropriate moment with him. Truthfully, at seven years his senior I was flattered by the attention.

In what was anticipated to be their best shot at me I was asked if I had ever been in therapy. I sat upright, and shouted: "The best money I ever spent!"

And I maintain to this day it WAS the best money I ever spent.

(More on this subject in part three)

In the final attempt to get me to break down, I was asked: "What made me think I was entitled to anything of my parents' estate?"

I answered that I wasn't entitled to any of my parents' estate, but neither were any of my siblings. No one is "entitled" to anyone else's stuff. I AM an heir, a beneficiary to my Mother's estate because I am her daughter, whom she loved and took definitive – specific steps to protect and to share her precious things with. That's called a gift—NOT an entitlement."

At the end of my deposition (which cost me more than $10,000 in attorney and travel fees) I was "ordered" to share notes, points I had written down (while being questioned for hour after hour) I had hoped to make for the record. My brothers' attorneys attempted to bully me into giving them my notes. Both my attorneys objected strenuously. I followed their lead and said, "No." As the screaming escalated demanding I comply, I stood up and walked out, but not before telling them they could "shove it up their asses!" (I was never instructed I could not make notes during my deposition)

No one bothered telling me my 5-hour deposition was "legally" not over until the opposing lawyers had dismissed me. Since I had "stormed out" before that happened, they considered my deposition invalid.

My attorneys shared that the opposing lawyers had planned all along to provoke me to erupt.

I'm not sorry I walked out.

I had been tormented my whole life and I had reached my limit.

I retreated to the ladies' room and vomited.

32

BUILDING MY CASE

In the following months, additional depositions were taken, this time, by my attorneys as we continued to prepare for trial to recover my ranch. My third brother, the "Golden Boy," was first.

(For the record, I retained written as well as audio accounts of the following depositions. The quotes are actual, sworn testimony taken under oath).

My brother, by his own admission, admitted he had been sued "many times before." This wasn't his first time being deposed. He knew how the game was played. He knew how to evade answering questions honestly and completely. Sarcasm was the cornerstone for humor with my siblings. It was rooted in the notion that being a smart aleck, putting others down by condescension, you could achieve some perceived level of superiority.

When questioned about his work history he began each sentence with, "I took a job..." repeating the pattern three times. Never once did he credit our Father who had arranged for each job. He exhibited no trace of humility or gratitude.

When my attorney asked, "If it was fair to say that your Dad was instrumental in assisting all of his (5) sons in getting car dealerships?" My brother answered, "No." My brother had perjured himself under oath several times giving much-needed ammunition to my attorney. I knew the truth, even so, it was unsettling to hear a liar in action.

When questioned about his relationship with Mom my brother insisted, they were "very close," stating that "We, (brothers #2 and #3) hired new counsel on behalf of my Mother to reconstruct her trust, her will, removing brother #5 for brother #2." This quote was significant because it proved what my Mother said was true. She NEVER hired the lawyer they chose and paid to change her will in favor of them. It also proves my brothers' attorney deliberately removed my Mom's (tangible) personal property sheets giving Her jewelry ONLY to her two daughters, and no one else.

This solidifies the fact that an attorney, chosen and paid by my brothers, was in-fact representing their interests IN DIRECT OPPOSITION to my Mother's wishes. That's fraud, malpractice on the part of that attorney, and in my opinion elder abuse.

My brothers were using Mom's own money to pay a lawyer to restructure her will to benefit themselves. How reprehensible.

*****

The final questions for my brother involved my ranch.

My brother TESTIFIED THAT MY DAD ONLY "LET [SUSAN] LIVE THERE." HE ADMITTED THAT HE HAD NEVER DISCUSSED WITH MOM AND DAD THE CIRCUMSTANCES UNDER WHICH I WAS RESIDING AT THE RANCH. HE ADMITTED THAT AFTER FINDING THE WARRANTY DEED SIGNED BY MOM, WHICH GIFTED THE RANCH TO SUSAN HE "REMOVED THE DEED" AND "NEVER DISCUSSED IT" WITH MOM. He testified that he HAD CALLED ME (SUSAN) TO QUESTION ME ABOUT THE DEED. THAT WAS A LIE. THAT NEVER HAPPENED. HE TESTIFIED THAT HE HAD IN HIS POSSESSION THE ORIGINAL WARRANTY DEED (stolen property) BELONGING TO SUSAN. At this point, my brother's attorney stated that he would not turn the deed over to my counsel "under any circumstances." In effect, this attorney agreed to continue to harbor stolen property. I did not know that lawyers could do that and get away with it. When asked under oath if he had "ever informed Susan of the existence of this warranty deed," he answered, "NO."

My brothers' intention was to gain possession of my ranch for himself by extricating his own sister. This would have infuriated my Mother. He admitted he never told Susan he had (stolen) the deed.

When asked why he had hired lawyers to begin eviction procedures against his sister, my brother said, and this is his exact quote, "The intent to evict was kind of an olive branch, if you would, to open up communication lines, because your client (Susan) was not talking to anyone in the family." My attorney questioned, "So your intent in trying to evict Susan was to get her to talk with you?" His answer: "Yeah." When asked if he had ever contacted Susan to discuss the eviction with her, he answered, "No." I believe those words speak for themselves.

Before my brother's deposition was over, he distorted numerous additional facts. He admitted to stealing two deeds from Mom's home six months BEFORE her death. They were the quick claim deeds to my ranch.

After testifying he never read the deeds and had no idea what they were, he divulged he took them across the country, recorded the one deed but kept the other for himself.

The first deed transferred my ranch from both my parent's names into my Mother's trust. That first deed my brother had recorded in my county. The second deed Mom signed transferring the ranch from my Mother's trust to me (Susan), never reached me. My brother admitted never "delivering" it or recording it for Susan. He kept it for himself.

When my attorney asked him if he was aware that the two deeds he removed from his Mother's home were "related" to Susan's ranch, he answered, "No." Then how did he know which deed to record?

He also revealed he never told his Mother he had taken her deeds.

I saw the deed only once and witnessed my Mother's signature in blue ink that brief 5 minutes I was on the stand the previous year.

That was as close as I ever got to the deed to my ranch.

33

ATTORNEYS LYING UNDER OATH

In preparation for trial, additional depositions were scheduled for two of my aunts, who corroborated my parents' reason for buying the ranch. "We bought the dealerships for the boys, we bought the ranch for Susie," both aunts repeating Mom's words. That same refrain was repeated by the previous owner who sold the ranch to my parents twenty years before. I was grateful for their support.

The final deposition was my youngest brother's, attorney who had referred to me as the family "freeloader" previously. He was the primary reason we were going to trial. He had prepared the two deeds but refused to "deliver" them to me so they could be legally recorded—this allowed the opportunity for my brother (#3) to steal the deeds from Mom's house—while she was still alive.

This attorney I'll refer to as "Mr. A. H." (You can fill in his initials) questioned Susan's "ability to run a ranch." So, after successfully running farms and ranches (along with my own career in advertising) for more than thirty years, my capabilities were being challenged by a used car salesman and an attorney who wouldn't know a gelding from a steer or alfalfa from straw. How insulting! Strange isn't it that never once did these same attorneys question my brother's ability to successfully run a car dealership without our parents' frequent million-dollar bailouts.

Mr. A. H. testified that my Mother had objected to his proposal to only give Susan "Part and not all" of the ranch.

On page 95 of his deposition (which I still have), he stated that my "Mother had decided NOT to make the gift" (of the ranch to Susan).

In a handwritten note to his lawyer (Mr. A. H.) his client, #5, wrote, "Dad and Mom's intention was that Sue would never be forced off the property." This attorney, (Mr. A. H.) knew Susan had received an eviction demand by her brother (#3) but did nothing to stop it.

Toward the end of questioning Mr. A. H. admitted his client (#5) had "stolen, misappropriated, lost—from nine to twelve million dollars in family assets since his Father's death."

To suggest that the attorneys representing my brothers had deliberately refused to follow the letter of the Law in executing our parents' wishes for their estate, is the understatement of all time.

I never realized until I witnessed it for myself, that so many attorneys, 'officers of the court' were willing to lie under oath to get their desired results for their clients, (my brothers).

Lying under oath is perjury. Perjury is considered a crime against justice because our system cannot FUNCTION PROPERLY if people continually lie in court.

To prove perjury, you must prove someone intentionally lied under oath, but how do you prove that? I had eyewitness testimonies, swearing before God, and man, my Mother's true intentions for "Susan's ranch."

The opposition attorneys, who NEVER even met or spoke to my Mother, called it "hearsay" dismissing my entire argument with no proof of their own.

Did you know that lying under oath is very RARELY prosecuted? I was shocked! Perjury convictions are rare, which to me, gives a green light to every dishonest person, "officer of the court" or normal citizen, willing to lie for personal gain.

Any wonder why normal people no longer believe a justice system exists in America any longer? When our judicial system cannot properly function without the truth when lying under oath is rarely punished, a system once rooted in truth and justice no longer exists.

34

THE OPEN HOUSE

Two and half years after my Mother died, I received a letter from a good friend of my late parents who still lived not far from my Mother's home. In a large manila envelope, she included newspaper clippings from the local paper. She was very upset. Did I know that my Mother's home was soon to be open to the public? Was I aware of what my brothers were up to? Since secrecy was always part of whatever schemes my brothers were involved in, I had no idea that my Mom's house would be open to the world. Thinking that total strangers could buy a ticket and roam the rooms of my Mother and Father's dream home made me hit the roof. My parents would have killed their sons for this prank. They were extremely private people and they NEVER would have approved of this shameless sales tactic.

The deal my brothers (2 and 3) struck was allowing local interior designers to redecorate the mansion however they wished to showcase the house and garner ticket sales for the local symphony. This was the brainstorm of a realtor who thought people buying an eight-dollar ticket might be willing to shell out another six million dollars to buy the home. As an heir, let alone a grieving daughter, I was never informed about this open house idea. Plus, I still had no idea where my brothers and their wives had hidden my Mother's personal possessions. Now, more than three years since her death.

One thing was certain. My brothers gave no thought to and had no respect for my parent's wishes, alive or dead. What would they do next? Open Mom's coffin and sell tickets? Could this stunt be another used car salesman's attempt to sell just one more "unit" to make a quota?

By the time the open house occurred I was still forbidden to enter my own Mother's home unless, of course, I paid $8 and waited in line with the tourists. My own law firm attempted to stop the open house but failed. My brothers and their realtor also failed. Multi-millionaires looking to buy oceanfront mansions do not buy tickets for some contrived house tour. In the end, I was proven right. The house did NOT sell as a result of the open house. More than eighteen months later I learned that house finally sold for half the asking price. It sold for its actual value. My brothers made sure that I never saw one dime from the sale of my Mother's home, which reportedly sold for around three and a half million dollars.

35

MY ROLEX WATCH

After learning (through his attorney's deposition) that my youngest brother had taken anywhere from two to twelve million dollars to save his failing dealership, we discovered that the automaker-corporation was about to file criminal charges against him. All six of #5's siblings were sent certified letters asking us to release money the local District Attorney wanted to drop the Indictment. The amount was $75,000. To be paid by the trust. All my siblings (four out of the five with arrest records of their own) voted "No." I voted "Yes" because my brother had little children (boy-girl twins) I never wanted to see go to jail.

My brother's lawyer testified EVERY sibling had voted no—another lie under oath that discredited Susan. Eventually, I learned that our brother (#3) was willing to allow (#5) the $75k in exchange for the deed to his $600,000 home. Hardly a fair trade, besides the fact that my brother's wife was divorcing him, and he owed her share of the equity in their home.

My brother knew I had voted on his behalf from the registered letter I had sent and told me I was the only one who had. That broke my heart. I knew he had been jailed at one point and was struggling to feed his family.

I was spending so much of what I made on legal fees the best I could offer to help my baby brother financially was the only decent piece of jewelry I ever owned: my Rolex watch. It had been a gift I treasured. I sent the watch, with my brother's favorite childhood homemade cookies I made, and waited for a response.

Weeks later when I finally reached him, I asked if he had received my watch? His response was, "You didn't need that watch." Not a thank you. Nothing.

Years later I learned my baby brother agreed to testify against me in the trial to recover my ranch. He had struck a deal with brothers #2, 3, and 4 to evict me.

So much for being my favorite brother.

He never spoke to me again.

36

THE IRS

For years my attorneys had filed endless motions in court to produce documents to which I was entitled as an heir. Time and time again my brothers and their attorneys refused to release crucial estate tax documents as a way of maintaining their power base. My brother (#5) by now in serious legal and financial trouble, was losing his home, his business, and his wife. Though brothers #2 and #3 had been named the personal representative of Mom's estate, #5 still controlled valuable estate assets including the limited family partnership money that Dad had set up years earlier tethering all seven children together.

As general manager of the partnerships, #5 paid the taxes on interest and dividends earned by the invested money. This was his legal obligation. But once he got into financial trouble—he had even been arrested, jailed, and indicted on criminal charges—he simply stopped paying the IRS. This situation created huge tax issues for his siblings, who were named in the family partnerships. For years his CPAs, were unwilling to distribute the information and IRS forms necessary to file a complete tax accounting by the April 15th deadline. For nearly a decade, I was forced to amend every IRS return as soon as his firm released the documents, usually by the October deadline. This created tax problems for me when I had never had any previous difficulty with the IRS.

From year to year, I never knew how much money I would have to come up with when these K-1 forms materialized. When I asked my brother if I owed any taxes from the partnership income, he always said, "No, the money is tax-free." My lawyer even agreed with this assessment. It wasn't until I got a letter from the IRS that I realized that I had to get to the bottom of, yet another mess created by my brother's shady accounting practices.

Because secrecy was so deep-seated in my family, I was tired of being denied access to information that I needed to provide to my own CPA. I decided to hire a tax attorney to help me. But where would I start?

I tried to get assistance from a cousin on the West Coast who was a tax attorney and a judge. She was unwilling to help. Another East Coast (lawyer) cousin who specialized in Wills and Trusts refused my calls. I began to wonder if selfish genes ran through the bloodlines of my family. Door after door slammed in my face.

Finally, a friend recommended a local female attorney who specialized in Tax Law. I liked her immediately upon entering her office because her tiny puppy, Peanuts, ran past the reception desk to greet me. Relieved, I felt I was in good company: a critter lover. She did not disappoint me. She had connections with the IRS and we managed to get the family partnership tax problems solved. Though it cost me a fortune in taxes, which I essentially was not responsible for, the situation also alerted the IRS to the way my brothers were mishandling Mom's estate. The IRS then did a forensic audit of Mom's Estate. "This became a year long excuse for my brothers to continue to refuse to distribute Mom's personal property." And, of course, the audit was deemed "Susan's fault" because I had jumped in to try and solve the partnership tax mess.

At the time of Mom's death, every American had a one-million-dollar personal exemption from estate taxes. All of Mom's personal tangible property fell under that million-dollar mark, so there was no legal reason why her things could not be distributed as she had instructed in her will. The IRS had no jurisdiction over Mom's personal things. It took months before my lawyers found out that #3 was earmarking Mom's personal exemption to reimburse him and certain other siblings for their own children's private educations. This would have infuriated Mom if she had still been alive.

Mom had been paying $6,000 per semester, per child, for my sister's kids to attend a private prep school. She wasn't the only one to hit Mom up for tuition. Mom had verbalized to me, time after time, that she thought it should be the parents' obligation to educate their children, not hers. Now her richest son, #3, was setting aside Mom's personal exemption for the use of beneficiaries who ostensibly would not pay to educate their own children. Being childless, I was excluded as a beneficiary from this money.

Additionally, Dad had told me before he died that he had bought a "lasting of living" insurance policy on Mom in the amount of $9,000,000 specifically to pay the IRS estate/death tax. After Mom's death, this money disappeared into thin air. No accounting was ever presented. My brothers all pointed fingers at each other. The only certain thing I knew was that Mom never touched that money and neither did I. So, I concluded, one of my brothers must have.

$9,000,000 gone.

37

SIX AGAINST ONE

A few days before Thanksgiving, three and a half years after Mom's death, a judge finally ordered my brothers to distribute my Mother's tangible personal property. This event was to occur across the country in a couple days. I objected. It was Thanksgiving week. Trying to make last-minute travel arrangements would be arduous. Additionally, I was a rancher with livestock to care for, which especially in winter, could be challenging. Trying to find a capable caretaker in such short notice would be nearly impossible. My lawyer petitioned the judge to move the date back, which he did.

I dreaded this trip. I felt like a lamb being led to slaughter. For that reason, I took two steps to ensure a more palatable outcome. First, I hired an off-duty policeman to accompany me whenever I had dealings with my siblings, and second, I asked my cousin (the brother I should have had) to meet me across the country for this "distribution" encounter.

My brothers had a history of abusive behavior both physical as well as emotional, and I felt I needed protection.

The travel across country was a nightmare. My reservations routed me north to fly south landing me in a full-blown snowstorm.

Eight long hours later I met my cousin at our destination. Fortified by my cousin's faith in me—that I would survive this encounter with my hateful siblings, we prepared for the rough days ahead of us.

After Mom's death, my brothers and their wives took possession of everything Mom owned despite having no legal right to do so. (They had not been appointed executors at that point in time) But following the Rule of Law wasn't something that these people ever lost sleep over.

Mom's "leftover" possessions had been hidden in a warehouse for over three and a half years. The "distribution" at the warehouse consisted of items which had not been stolen by her sons.

It was a shock to see what little was left of my parents' fifty-year marriage.

As my cousin and I entered the huge warehouse, my sister and three brothers greeted my cousin. No one said a word to me.

All seven heirs were asked to submit a list of what they wanted from Mom's tangible personal property. Mom's personal list for the disbursement was stolen. Each heir was to provide the others' attorneys with their lists as ordered by the court. That never happened. I was never provided with anyone else's list. I was the only heir to comply with the court order.

I asked for relatively few items out of an 11,000 square foot mansion. A number of items I requested were gifts of art I had made for my parents. Also, the value of the majority of these items was minimal. I noted the items I knew had been "removed". Brazenly, my brothers stupidly admitted to stealing many items even though they knew that Mom had discussed exactly what she wanted for the distribution of her personal property with me prior to her death and put it into writing.

Once I arrived at the warehouse, the emotional tension showed. My siblings were furious at me for bringing my cousin along. Their level of abuse was going to be diminished by his presence. The only time I was spoken to was in anger or sarcasm.

I had picked up a statue of the Blessed Mother that my Father cherished. I was quietly reminiscing about watching Dad empty his suit pockets every night and putting his wallet, loose change and rosaries next to the statue. Dad always kissed the crucifix of his black rosary before he laid it at the feet of the Virgin Mary. Lost in memories, I was jolted back to reality when my brother (#3) yelled at me, "Don't touch anything." Rage edged his voice. His rebuke was hateful. No one else was chastised for touching. I could feel the hatred in that warehouse. I could see it in his eyes. He was scary, unstable.

I was watched like a hawk. I was treated like a criminal. #3 found it very difficult to contain his animosity toward me. At times he had to physically remove himself from the warehouse to collect himself, with a cigarette and a drink.

The first day was to view items that remained and to list what we wanted. Day two was to hand our list to my brother (#3) who, in all his omnipotence, would decide who got what. As you can imagine this half-ass attempt to appropriate Mom's things met with resistance since many items had not been marked with a number code intended to speed up the process. There was no organization, and no communication making even the smallest decision monumental. Emotions were at a fever pitch and, as expected, any item I wanted was met with snickering and interference.

Since my cousin and I witnessed how emotionally fragile my brother (#3) running the show was, we thought it best to put my off-duty deputy on "Stand by." My cousin wisely ascertained my brother's frail demeanor would most likely erupt with the presence of a lawman.

As predicted little good came out of the "warehouse" experience except I was able to salvage a few items I knew Mom wanted me to have. While on a trip to Ireland Dad had bought Mom a complete (service for twelve) set of Waterford crystal glassware. It was "awarded" to me by my brother who reversed his own decision as my cousin was loading up our rented SUV with the crystal. I was chastised for removing more than he expected. When I reminded him Dad had bought Mom a service "for 12" he said he had promised "someone else" Mom's Waterford. He insisted Mom had two different patterns. She did not, and to prove it, I unboxed every piece of crystal on a table and challenged him to see for himself. In the process I counted 16 missing glasses to which he snapped, "Mom broke them." I told him that was a lie I could prove. I was to learn that the "someone else" he promised Mom's crystal to was a granddaughter not in Mom's will.

For the record, NONE of my Mother's eight daughters-in-law were in her will or trust. Neither were her grandchildren.

Principally Mom wanted her personal things to go to my sister and I. Her daughters, as is tradition. It did not matter to me that my brothers had already removed rooms full of furniture including widescreen TVs and electronics, kitchen appliances, computers, and tools.

What infuriated me was my brother's (#3) estranged wife had looted my Mother's (50-year) recipe collection. She often bragged she would one day take it, and she did.

I was a professional food stylist as part of my career in advertising. I had worked to prepare "perfect camera-ready" dishes for cookbooks as well as print media and TV commercials. I had worked for national clients such as Arby's, Hardees, Coca Cola as well as Coors.

It hurt me personally as well as professionally, not to have my resource—the recipe collection handwritten in Mom's unique script.

This was a violation of the Mother-daughter bond no daughter-in-law had a right to violate.

When I complained to my attorney about this infringement we were given "Xerox" copies of a limited number of recipes. I never saw my Mother's recipes again. This was their culinary finger salute to me.

As tensions mounted my cousin and I agreed that it was time to get the few items "awarded" me from the warehouse and get the hell out of there. It was evident the rules laid down by my brother never applied to any other family members except "Susan."

When I attempted to remove an oil painting I had been granted, my sister erupted with all the force of Mt. Vesuvius ordering me to put it back. When I showed her the number on the item corresponding to the number awarded me, she insisted the numbers had been switched, and my older brother (her ally) was taking both paintings by the same artist. By some unknown force, the accurate number had been switched to a group of Japanese silk prints I never chose.

I had been set up, and their laughter gave them away. I was the only artist in the family with two degrees and a successful career to prove it, but none of that mattered. They made certain I would not receive even one painting from a collection that included several.

When asked if I could take the original art I had painted for Mom and Dad, my brother's exact words were, "Take that shit. Nobody else wants it."

So I did. Several of my paintings were missing—most likely destroyed.

Sensing I had reached my breaking point my sister wasn't going to let me go without confronting me.

Within minutes my sister was out of control. "You're a Mother fucking bitch," she screamed.

"Why don't you calm down?" I asked as my brothers stood mute hoping for a catfight.

"Why should I? You're the one who keeps getting in the way. Even at Mom's funeral."

"At least I cared enough to eulogize Mom, to publicly say thanks to her for all she'd done for us."

My sister shot back, "AND WE ALL HATE YOU FOR THAT!"

She continued to shriek at me that our older brother (#1) was going to speak at Mom's funeral, but I apparently stole his moment by giving my eulogy. I answered back there was no rule only one eulogy could be given, and even if there had been, when did our family ever follow the rules? (Witnesses can confirm I WAITED before walking to the podium at Mom's funeral not knowing if some other family member had prepared a speech.) Even if they had, NO ONE was going to stop me from delivering the eulogy Mom herself asked me to give.

When my sister paused for air, I grabbed the opportunity—I did the unthinkable.

I said to my sister, "Go sober up."

THAT DID IT. As if propelled by some superhuman force, my sister leaped across a row of couches and bolted in my direction. Hoping to clean my clock my brothers did nothing to thwart her assault. By the time she reached me, I had locked my feet in a ninja stance, readying myself for battle. My sister pushed me, but my cousin stepped in front of me to stop her advance.

My cousin quickly ushered me into the rental car with the few remaining items I wanted, and we took off as my sister's screaming continued.

My cousin exclaimed, "Your siblings are sick. Totally sick!"

Not even a mile down the road my cousin's cell phone rang and we were ordered to return to the warehouse so my siblings could "inspect" what we had taken.

"HELL, NO WE ARE NOT GOING BACK THERE!" I screamed. My cousin called back and promised our inventory.

At that point, my cousin stated, "I guess we shouldn't have canceled the police protection, I never expected the assault to come from your sister."

Once safely back at our motel all I wanted was a hot bath and to get in my pajamas. My brothers and sister had invited our cousin to dinner, which was fine with me. I flipped him the rental car keys and said, "See you in the lobby for breakfast."

When I saw my cousin the following morning he was frothing at the mouth with anger. As expected, the entire evening had been a three-hour bitch session about "Susan."

"Susie, it's a miracle you've survived in your family."

I was glad my cousin witnessed that vitriolic attack on my character.

My cousin proclaimed, "Susie, no matter what you think they ended up with from your parent's estate—they have NOTHING. Nothing. Their lives are miserable. They are consumed with hate and revenge. They have NO idea who you are. They've created a monster that never existed so they could justify their stealing and hate. You have more going for you than they ever will have in all their lives put together."

Before leaving for home the next day, I drove my cousin by my parent's home —the house where my Mom was killed. We stood at the foot of the driveway and for the first time it hit me. They were gone.

Mom and Dad's spirits had left. It felt peaceful and good. In my heart, I believed my parents were giving me permission to let go, to move on with my own life, to stop looking back.

As the jet ascended, I felt relieved I had survived, thanks to my cousin, one of the worse experiences of my life. It felt as though I had rescued a small part of Mom and was bringing her home with me.

38

GOING THE DISTANCE

We were scheduled for the trial to begin to determine the true ownership of my ranch, in only days.

I received a call from my attorney which would change the course of my life. I held my breath as he stated—

"Your brother and his attorney said if we go to trial and you win, you will not receive your share of the millions he controls from the limited family partnership accounts. As the court-appointed personal representative, he will simply refuse to give your rightful inheritance."

I took a deep breath as he continued. "Also, your brother, along with your other siblings, will tie everything up on appeal for another four or five years. You will have to spend your own money, as you have been doing, to continue to pay your legal team. It would ruin you financially."

"My brother is not spending a dime out of pocket, is he? He's using the estate money to pay his legal bill."

"That's right," he said,

"IN ESSENCE I'M BEING BLACKMAILED INTO A SETTLEMENT, RIGHT?"

"YES."

That was it. I lost my ranch, my home of twenty years to blackmail.

"My family is going to deny my right to be heard, to tell my side of this story at trial, correct?' I said.

"I'm afraid so," he lamented.

I remember instructing my attorney with the words: "No more, it's over, I cannot continue, they win. Let's end this nightmare, now."

During the following days of negotiations, my lawyer called several times. Perceptively he announced, "Susan, you are right. Your brother IS a god in his own world. Everyone is scared to death of him."

To say I was unimpressed with my attorney's negotiating abilities would have been an understatement. He may have known legal procedure, but I believed he was incompetent as a negotiator. Despite his inability to achieve anything close to our initial agreement, he walked away with $600,000 of my inheritance. Sadly, he never even bought me a hamburger.

As a result of the settlement, I got only a small fraction of what I was entitled to as a beneficiary of my parent's estate. Millions of dollars of my parent's hard-earned money went to my brothers' attorneys and advisors and millions more were squandered by illegal business dealings by my brothers. I was denied a full and complete accounting of the thirty-million-dollar estate.

In the end, Dad was proven right. He had good reason not to trust his sons to manage then distribute his and Mom's estate.

Now it was time for me to move on and begin a new life no longer tethered to the corrupt element, which was my former family.

*****

A few days later I got a call from a cousin across the country. She and her husband had always been supportive of me. My sister, who NEVER had a relationship with this cousin, called to tell her my brother (#3) "Forced her, and the remaining family members, into signing a document instructing that NO ONE was ever to speak to Susan again for the duration of their lives. That's a quote."

My cousin was shocked by what she heard. I was smart enough to know this was my brother's juvenile attempt to make sure "Susan" got word she was no longer considered a member of my parents' family.

I was once Aunt Susie to (18) nieces and nephews, and now, I understand, a great aunt as well. For a woman who could never have children, I found this particularly cruel.

39

THE FINAL INSULT

Mom had her own private reasons for cherishing her jewelry as her most prized worldly possession. It symbolized for Mom and Dad all they had overcome in their life together since World War II. As newlyweds when they struggled to build their future together Dad's private joke was that someday he would have Mom "Dripping in diamonds." Mom would smile then go wash another dirty diaper.

When Dad finally made it big, he kept his promise to Mom by buying her beautiful jewelry, most of which he proudly designed himself.

A lady in the most traditional sense of the word, Mom never left the house without being impeccably groomed and wearing something stunning from her jewelry collection. This was her crowning glory. It was her kiss from Dad even long after he was gone. She had earned the right to wear diamonds and other precious gems. She always looked like a queen and I was proud of her for that.

I never coveted my Mother's jewelry. I don't believe my sister did either. But my brothers' wives did.

Mom cringed when her sons' wives brazenly declared openly which rings, bracelets or necklaces they coveted. This outraged my Mother. Mom seethed with anger at these greedy, arrogant, spoiled women who assumed rank, privilege, and possessions to which they were not entitled simply by marrying into our family.

One of my Mother's biggest concerns was the emerging power these women wielded and what would happen to her personal jewelry collection. That is why she took definitive steps to ensure that her prized personal possessions would never go to her sons' wives or their children. If Mom stood in judgment of her daughters-in-law, she had good reason. One had abandoned her husband and infant children. One mysteriously "lost" twins, then had two children out of wedlock, and then married only to abandon her two small boys to become a topless dancer. One had multiple DUIs and several assault arrests. There were divorces and more divorces, most of which Mom and Dad paid for.

Mom could not stand these women who, for a time, had been married to her sons. She never considered them family. In Mom's mind, they had no right to her jewelry or any of her personal things. For that reason, Mom expressed in writing and verbally that she wanted her jewelry to go to her own two blood daughters and no one else. Mom never wavered on this point and everyone in the family knew it.

Her attorneys knew it too, she put it in writing.

In the end, my brother's (#3) wife had ultimate control over my Mother's jewelry. Just as my Mother feared, daughters-in-law and granddaughters were given priority over me. My sister was granted preferential treatment because she agreed to testify against me at my trial to recover my ranch. My sister was "awarded" every piece of jewelry she wanted.

Out of the fifty-seven choices available (not all of Mom's jewelry was recovered; some things had simply disappeared), I asked for four items. I was denied the first three things I asked for, including my Mother's wedding rings, which I was entitled to as the eldest daughter. I was given a charm bracelet and an "I love you" bracelet that Dad had told everyone he wanted Susie to have. Two items that I had given Mom as gifts (a sapphire cross and a platinum diamond snowflake pin) were returned to me but counted as my choices. Then I was told I could have a ring, bracelet, earrings and necklace on loan. I am not allowed to keep these items. Upon my death they must be returned to my brother's wife. Right.

Any chance in hell of that happening?

I was refused a court-ordered accounting of how my Mother's jewelry was distributed. Upon hearing about the outcome of Mom's jewelry her only sister cried, "Your brother raped his own Mother," which accurately summed up how I felt.

It was "assumed" I would not share Mom's jewelry when I had no daughters of my own. My right, my position in the family, by all traditional rights, should have insured my participation in distributing my own Mother's jewelry.

Even that honor was taken from me and given to a gold-digger who claimed she never loved my brother and only married him for the money. Every fear Mom had was valid and justified.

Once again, my sisters-in-law maliciously and deliberately violated the sacred bond between my Mother and me.

I leave you with one question:

If these eight sisters-in-law believed they were entitled to my Mother's

jewelry—then why wasn't I entitled to THEIR Mothers' jewelry?
　　I rest my case.

To this day I have NEVER once worn one piece of my Mother's jewelry. NEVER ONCE. Why? Because the disrespect my brothers and their wives so tyrannized me with rendered what few items I received as emotionally damaged goods.
　　Not only did they steal my Mother's most precious gift to me, they stole any joy I could have felt while wearing it.
　　To me, that's unforgivable.

PART THREE

Lessons Learned

40

THE AFTERMATH

Time and distance has not diminished the pain of my estate nightmare. I have lived with the familial betrayal and financial loss from the day I was blackmailed into settlement.

I have witnessed corruption, over the years, at the highest level of institutions I once considered sacrosanct. The Church, the government, the judicial system, as well as my own family.

Most people will never experience, nor can they imagine, the level of hate I encountered in the wake of my Mother's death.

Short of a bullet to my head (which my own attorney warned me about) the consensus of my team of attorneys was that my family's estate mess was the worst they had ever seen.

Unlike my siblings, who all had long histories with the judicial system, I did not.

What I learned over time I wanted to share with you in the hope you will never endure the verbal abuse, the gender discrimination, the fraud, stealing, betrayal, blackmail, as well as threats from my brothers' attorneys.

They say experience is the best teacher. If that is true, I consider myself an expert at surviving an estate nightmare.

My hope in sharing my story is to shed some light on issues seldom talked about and rarely addressed. Levels of corruption in the legal system which make it impossible for the average citizen, without deep pockets, to pursue justice on any level.

I no longer believe in a "Justice" system once intended to protect the innocent and most vulnerable among us. What I now believe in is a "Legal" system where corruption is rampant, and attorneys fear no retaliation in committing perjury under oath.

My hope in sharing the wisdom I gained through my experience is to help you avoid the heartbreaks and legal expense before it ever comes to that.

What I am sharing is preventative steps to help educate you to avoid problems involving end of life issues.

Looking back, I am proud I stood up against tyranny. I was outnumbered, out financed and out-gunned. There is no shame in losing when you have fought evil legally, ethically and morally.

Unlike our Father, not one of my brothers would die a hero.

41

IF YOUR LEGACY MATTERS TO YOU

If your family matters to you, get a Will done NOW. Do not put it off because you don't believe you have much of an estate or because you don't think you are that old. The cemeteries are full of people who were not ready or prepared to die. Take the time and put in the effort and expense to do it right. It is the most important and unselfish thing you will ever do for your children or your heirs. Be as specific as you need to be. Getting a will done is not for the weak of heart. It takes courage to face end of life issues. It takes courage to make decisions about your estate and your money. Some of your choices might anger your heirs but remember that it is YOUR life, and these are your choices. You are entitled to call in the debts owed to you. You are entitled to decide who gets your property, home, vehicles, furnishings, collections, personal clothing, and jewelry. Most importantly, you are entitled to choose who will raise your underage children.

You have rights that you would never give up in life. Why would you give them up in death? If you do not decide what will happen to your estate, someone else will decide for you. Judging from the statistics, the odds of your wishes being carried out without a will are slim. The will is the only legal instrument that can carry out your wishes after your death and it needs to be prepared in a careful and thoughtful manner. Be diligent and cover all the bases. A detailed estate plan needs to be bulletproof so that your heirs will never have to suffer the enormous financial burden of litigation, in addition to the emotional loss of losing their loved one.

42

MONEY

There would have been no need for me to tell this story if the men mentioned in this book (aside from my Father) had been of honorable character. Contrary to public belief, fortunes do not make a man, they expose him.

The ruthless pursuit of someone else's money revealed the true content of those men's (and women's) hearts. In the Gospel according to St. Matthew, we are instructed, "Where your heart is, so is your fortune." It was no coincidence that Jesus spoke more about money than any other issue. Is money the root of all evil? No. But the love of money, an obsession with money, is evil. Money is necessary, but there is a great deal that money cannot buy.

> Money cannot buy love or respect.
> Money cannot buy good health or longevity.
> Money cannot buy good character.
> Money cannot buy happiness.
> Money cannot buy peaceful resolutions to problems.
> Money cannot buy a harmonious family life.

Most of us are confused about what money can and cannot buy. A lottery winner once proclaimed that now that he had money, he would have a "perfect life." What a foolish remark! What an unrealistic expectation he put on money. Money does not bring satisfaction or fullness in our lives. Those are spiritual qualities deep within each of us. Until we realize that we are primarily spiritual beings, then money, and all the things it can buy for us, will always fall short of making us happy. There is only so much money can do. It has limitations. Most of us, unfortunately, refuse to acknowledge that.

My siblings equated wealth with worth. Because they were handed money by our parents, they began to believe that they were more successful, more worthy, more valuable than others. Because I had no wealth (in comparison to them) they concluded that I had little worth as a person. My brother, the executor, once stated in front of my employees, "I'll decide what you get." In an attempt to limit the amount of inheritance my parents had left me. Additionally, another brother once told my attorney, "Susan is single. She has no children and no heirs, she doesn't deserve any inheritance."

When issues arise that pit someone's character against money, the true nature of a man (or woman) is revealed. Someone with poor character is generally incapable of managing money well. People who cannot control their money cannot control their lives, and vice versa. They have no reality checks. They are undisciplined and unrealistic. They often buy and buy and buy more things in order to feel valuable, or important. That is the main reason why credit debt is out of control in our country.

The bottom line is unless you are a person of good character you are going to have a proclivity to worship money. In the event of someone's death, an executor's propensity towards money could lead that person into unethical, immoral, even illegal means of attaining easy money which was never intended to be theirs. This is why it is essential, that you look at the issues of character and money together. Choose an executor who is of impeccable character. Without character, money will destroy the person who attains it, legally or illegally.

43

RECIPE FOR A HEALTHY ESTATE PLAN

1. The right person or persons with the highest character is chosen as executor
2. All beneficiaries/heirs are treated with consideration and respect
3. All heirs are given the same information at the same time
4. Female heirs are not discriminated against in any way
5. Estate advisors should respect all heirs
6. Estate advisors should never be in collusion with the executor or selected heirs to make sweetheart deals, steal documents, withhold information, or be disrespectful to the remaining heirs
7. The value and assets of the estate are disclosed to ALL the heirs to eliminate any veil of secrecy
8. The matriarch or patriarch (verbally and in written form) discloses any family debts owed to the estate. These loans must be documented.
9. In-laws must respect the boundaries of the nuclear family. They should respectfully keep quiet and keep their hands in their own pockets.
10. Grandchildren are not considered direct heirs unless specifically mentioned in the Will. Parents are not obligated to secure them a stash. Genetics does not mean they are entitled to anything. Avoid expectations. They often create enormous problems within a family, not to mention non-family members, including in-laws and friends.
11. Advisors must work together with the family to mitigate any disagreements.

Because people are fallible, some estate problems are inevitable. But there is no reason why so many of them have to fail.

44

CHOOSING AN EXECUTOR

Remember this point: when you choose your executor or personal representative you are granting them every right and privilege you possess to your property, to everything you own. This is not supposed to be a license to steal. But that does not guarantee that the person won't steal, won't take advantage of you and your heirs.

It is the executor's job to settle the estate and distribute the assets in the best interest of the beneficiaries according to your will. Alexander A. Bove writes in *Wills, Estates, and Trusts* that "the law does not demand a high standard for the position of executor. Anyone can be named as an executor." Red flags should be flying frantically here. Why don't we have higher standards for those people allowed to settle estates?

Until I started my research, it never occurred to me that the courts have very few standards for choosing executors. On page twenty-one of Alexander A. Bove's *The Complete Book of Wills, Estates, and Trusts*, he states, "Generally, you may not appoint a minor, or incompetent person, or in many states, a convicted criminal. Otherwise, the appointment will not be rejected even if the person is extremely old, or suffers from a handicap, or has no business experience, *or is a heavy drinker, or is a creditor of the estate*, or a witness to the will, or a beneficiary, or is thought to be mental or morally impure."

I learned from experience that this is true. My attorney explained that it is extremely difficult to have an executor removed once legally appointed by the courts. When I went to court and testified that my brothers were incapable of fairly distributing our Mother's estate, the judge disregarded my pleas and appointed them anyway. The judge imposed a $2,000,000 bond on both brothers for anything they "might have stolen or might still steal" from the estate. This was the court's attempt to say, "We're watching you, so don't steal anything." Unfortunately this deterrent was futile.

We all knew that the stealing had long been in progress, even prior to my Mother's death, and no bond was going to stop it. Recovery of missing assets was nearly impossible and would have cost me a fortune in detective and legal fees. My attorney told me that these court-imposed bonds would force my brothers to return stolen property from Mom's estate, including hundreds of thousands of dollars' worth of jewelry. That never happened. Who was going to hold them accountable and how much would that have cost? One of the great disappointments that I was forced to face was that my attorneys were unwilling to fight for the return of stolen items. They simply didn't think it was that big a deal. Maybe it was a gender difference, but I believe most women would understand my need to retrieve personal items belonging to my Mother, which she intended only for her two daughters.

It shocked me that our judicial system refuses to see Alcoholism as a viable reason for refusal to appoint a candidate as executor. If you cannot trust a drunk behind the wheel of your car how can you trust them with everything you have accumulated in your lifetime? How can you trust them with your children?

Judges may know Law, but they certainly don't know addiction. I was appalled at the legal system which gives a green light to grave robbing, because appointing an addict to distribute an estate is just that. It is like giving John Gotti the keys to Fort Knox and telling him not to steal.

I have come to the conclusion that it is generally best to choose an executor who is not a family member for the simple reason that too many (family) executors begin to believe that the estate really belongs to them and not the deceased person. Their new position as the individual "in charge" puts too much of a strain on the remaining family members. Unless there is trust among all the siblings involved, resentment is inevitable when issues arise which are not agreed upon by all family members. In my family situation, trust was nonexistent. Punitive retaliation became necessary because my brothers actually began believing that Mom and Dad's fortune was theirs. None of my brothers had the most important ingredient necessary to succeed as an executor: character.

Unless the family member has a sterling character, I'm against an immediate family member as an executor. There may be an uncle or aunt or cousin who might make an objective executor, but no matter who is chosen, their character must be scrutinized. Most sibling executors fail in their objectives for impartial distribution. The problem of objective, fair, compassionate, equal treatment of all the heirs manifests itself when favorable treatment for some is countered with harsh, punitive treatment for others.

Childhood grudges, greedy in-laws, lazy alcoholics, vindictive addicts, jealous wives, may lie in wait, many for decades, for the opportunity to get even with the siblings they have always despised. A will is the perfect venue for revenge.

It takes great courage to choose the right executor for an estate. Don't forget that this is YOUR will; these are YOUR things. This is about YOUR money and everything you own. You decide, and no one else, how your estate is to be distributed. When choosing my own executor, I chose the one person who possessed the most important quality I considered necessary for that position: Character.

Afterthought: I cannot emphasize enough the dangerous thinking many (family) executors begin to believe once they assume the role of executor—that it's now THEIR money.
It is not.
It is still your parent's property which should be distributed to their heirs the way THEY wished.

If the person you have in mind for the serious position of executor (or trustee) doesn't have the character to respect his parent's wishes—and follow them—please choose someone else who will!

45

CHOOSING AN EXECUTOR WITH CHARACTER

When most of us hear psychiatric terms to describe someone's behavior in terms of good or bad character, we don't often identify anybody we know, let alone love. Until that spouse leaves us for another, or a sibling cleans out our bank account, or a friend cons us into loaning them money, which they have no intention of repaying, we will never see the evil around us. Until we've been grievously wronged, we are often not willing to look at the dark side of a person's character. Of course, by then, it is often too late to remedy the situation.

How can we test a person's character? I have two answers: stress and time. We are all tested in times of stress. The difference between a good person and an evil person becomes evident in the way they handle stress. People of integrity never desert their values, their responsibilities, or their maturity. They remain respectful and sensitive to the needs of others. In contrast, people with evil character traits blame others for their pain. They are arrogant, selfish, and lazy. They are chronic liars. They lack courage. They are weak and untrustworthy. They constantly run to anything that will relieve their pain, which usually results in addiction (recognize anyone you know?)

Evil people don't see themselves as the root of their problems, so they see no need to grow or change. They become perpetual victims. They always take the easy way out. They lack discipline and they hate it in others. Because they are obsessed with power, they must be in control at all times. And, they act alone except for the people they coerce into their game. They are not team players.

Remember this: TIME always reveals a man's character. A person's pattern of behavior over time is the best determinate of his REAL qualities and values.

After the anguish I suffered at the hands of the men who commandeered my Mother's estate, I believe the most important decision you can make is the choice of executor/trustee of your will. Incredibly, not one of the men chosen by my parents had the character to carry out their instructions as they had wished.

At this stage in my life, I have come to classify people into two categories: those with character and those with character disorders. I have told numerous stories in this book describing people with character disorders.

You don't need a "PhD" to recognize people capable of making your life, or the lives of your loved ones, a living hell.

A personality disorder is a way of thinking or behaving that deviates from the normal—rational expectations in our culture.

After my Father died I decided to go into therapy to better understand how my family worked and how to survive. Once I spilled my guts to my therapist for two hours, I asked him what I was doing wrong and how could I fix it? He looked at me and said, "Susan, there isn't a damn thing wrong with you, you're in a dysfunctional, narcissistic, selfish, and alcoholic family!"

Therapy wasn't meant to continue for the rest of my life, so I was determined to make the most of it while I could. I was introduced to information I was starving to discover. I began reading and studying every self-help book I could get my hands on—on subjects ranging from alcoholism, to narcissism, to addictions of every kind, to character, to adultery to workaholism. What I learned was a lot. I couldn't get enough information into my head. I was absorbing knowledge like a sponge.

Additionally, I started reading my Bible again after decades, and, amazingly I began to experience true WISDOM. (I believe all Wisdom comes from God).

In humbling myself to ask for help, I found that my "trifecta" of therapy, in combination with intense reading, along with ardent Bible study laid a foundation of knowledge that sustained me throughout the years of abuse I encountered once my protector, Dad, was gone.

Most of the characters I had encountered were stereotypical—men with an inflated sense of their own importance. Women who believed they deserved special treatment. Men who exaggerated their achievements who showed little regard for other's feelings. People who felt entitled to the best of everything. Individuals who were arrogant and pretentious. Thugs who were intellectually shallow who used mafia-style tactics to intimidate and frighten elderly women into submission for their own personal gain.

After sharing my estate nightmare I am certain you were able to tell the good guys from the bad guys.

Here's my advice:

Pick a good guy (or gal) for your executor.

The following list of questions may help you make a more informed decision:

> Are they honest?
> Are they respectful of women?
> Do they have a history of addiction?
> Do they pay their bills?
> Do they owe you money?
> Do they have a history of arrests?
> How do they treat their parents? Siblings?
> And finally, can you trust them?

Sadly, the son my Father trusted the least, (#3) became the son who took control of my parents' fortune and made sure he benefited the most.

I have come to the conclusion that TRUST in the family, or rather the LACK OF TRUST within the family is the single biggest reason why most wills fail.

If the family member who becomes executor is the least trustworthy person within the family, it's only a matter of time before the family will implode. It's inevitable.

To eliminate the possibility of that happening I would choose a person who doesn't bring with them a history of resentments and prejudices—a non-family member.

Someone trusted, of fine character, who can objectively carry out the duties as executor without the emotional baggage a close family member would inexorably have.

And finally, trust your gut instincts. If someone is actively campaigning to be named your executor—that's a major red flag. You should feel comfortable and confident in your choice as executor.

If you don't, that's a sign you may be making one of the biggest mistakes of your life.

You deserve better.

So does your family.

Choosing the best person as your executor takes courage, so, step up to the plate and give it all you've got.

You've got nothing to lose, but your loved ones have everything to gain.

Good luck!

46

BEWARE OF GENDER DISCRIMINATION

In my opinion, the biggest single reason why my Mother's estate was not protected and distributed according to her wishes was that the men who controlled her estate had a blatant disrespect for women. These men made no secret of their gender bias. They simply ignored my Mother's written and verbal instructions. These men attempted to devalue me in the same way.

It is a fact that most wives outlive their husbands. It only follows that most women will inherit the bulk of a family estate. When estate transfers (wills) do not work successfully, you can bet that one of the major reasons is that the wishes of widows have not been recognized and respected. The men associated with my Mother in her later years, including her own sons, simply saw her an obstacle to a fortune they coveted for themselves. They had no desire to follow the directives of an elderly matriarch. So they didn't. It was easy to use the legal system arena as a place to hide information and stolen documents. All they had to do was manipulate and control then wait for the "old gal" to die.

To say that gender discrimination does not exist within the legal profession is to ignore the obvious. Many men, including spouses, brothers, and attorneys, simply will never accept women as equals. If you are female, no matter what your relationship is with a male, you had better take steps to protect yourself and your estate. Invest a great deal of time in interviewing and choosing advisors who are respectful and who reflect and will represent your personal values. Choose only those professionals with a proven track record. Choose ones you can trust. Never allow others with hidden agendas to choose advisors for you as my Mother was forced into doing before she died.

47

FAILING THE BAR

Prior to my family's estate nightmare, I believed in our legal system. I had confidence the courts would protect my legal rights as an heir. I was wrong. I once believed lawyers were paid to solve problems. I was wrong. Most of the lawyers I encountered were paid to create problems, NOT solve them.

In her book, *The Case Against Lawyers,* Catherine Crier, herself a lawyer and a judge, writes, "The rule of law has become a source of power and influence, not liberty and justice." Many lawyers pledged to justice and democracy for the good of all the people deliberately do not work toward those goals. What motivates a lawyer to ignore the laws of society? The answer is not surprising: Money.

In the eyes of the public, many lawyers have betrayed their sacred oath to uphold the laws, to fight for the rights of all men and women, and to put justice before personal advancement and wealth. People are smart. They know right from wrong and moderation from excess. Most Americans see lawyers as elitists who have written a very difficult code of laws with language designed to manipulate the system intended to protect everyman. Laws are a necessary part of a civilized society. The problems begin when truth and justice no longer become the attorney's goals, but financial gain does.

When my attorney complained bitterly after he discovered that my brother's attorney billed my Mother's estate for $86,000 for only one month's work, then refused to disclose what those charges represented, no one cared.

When another attorney, who never met me, referred to me as the "The family freeloader," no one cared.

When property deeds, signed by my Mother, legally giving me my ranch, were never "delivered" or "recorded" by her own attorney resulting in the loss of my home, business and ranch, no one cared. The following are a few points I learned along the way to help you learn the legal process:

My inexperience as well as my Mother's with the legal system gave my brothers' attorneys enormous advantages. I was unfamiliar with the legalese language so it was easy for them to intimidate me. A good attorney will explain the legal terminology. For clarification see *1001 Legal Words You Need to Know* by Jay M. Feinman.

It is not often in a lawyer's best interest to expedite any legal procedure. The longer the dispute lasts, the more they get paid.

You must be proactive in your case. Keep notes, files, documents, letters, correspondence, copies which could help your attorney win your case. Take notes. Ask questions. Make sure your attorney includes you in important discussions.

Lawyers get paid even if they lose your case. If they lose, they still win financially.

Don't be offended if your attorney is not as emotionally invested in your legal problem as you are. This is a job for them...NOT a relationship. He/she is not the one being hurt—you are.

In my opinion, men have more advantages in court proceedings. When the judge overturned his own ruling after awarding my ranch to a "single woman," would his decision be different had I been a single man? What do you think?

The more discord within your family, the happier many lawyers will be. Disharmony and disagreements tell unscrupulous lawyers to throw fuel on the fires of negotiations allowing the inferno to burn for weeks, months, years and often decades.

The longer the fire burns, the bigger their paycheck.

Moral character is not a requirement to earn a Law degree. Unethical attorneys take on clients every day who have criminal histories like my brothers. Water seeks its own level. Honest attorneys wouldn't represent addicts who lie, steal and cheat. Far too many lawyers have no problem taking advantage of a family in distress.

    Having had working relationships with several honest, ethical attorneys in the ensuing years, I am proud to admit that good lawyers do exist.
    Unfortunately, my family never hired any of them.

48

THE TRICKS EVIL LAWYERS PLAY

It didn't take much of an attorney to frighten an elderly widow and tyrannize her daughter for the purpose of stealing her property for his client. In refusing to execute my Mother's directives the attorneys hired by my brothers failed in their fiduciary duty to her. I have described several of the tactics they used to help you identify their strategies:

> Some lawyers will use the "divide everything equally" plan among heirs despite written, specific instructions that distribute personal tangible property. This means that despite outstanding loans, or financial obligations, by one or more family members owed the estate, their attorney will attempt to have those obligations dismissed so the remaining assets get divided "evenly", which means unevenly in reality. This cheats honest heirs out of substantial assets, which were never repaid by their siblings.

> Ignoring a client's direct request, without explanation, is another way to erode your control over your assets. Competent lawyers will always explain their strategy to you. By simply choosing to ignore your directive to transfer or distribute an asset, some attorneys may jeopardize the future of that asset. The best example I can give here was the refusal of my Mother's attorney to record and deliver the warranty deed(s) to me for my ranch. As a direct result of his action, or intentional "in action", my Mother's intent was never realized, and my ranch and studio were stolen from me.

> Some lawyers may align themselves with one or more beneficiaries for the purpose of creating illegal "Sweetheart Deals." This results in robbing the remaining heirs of the rightful

value of a particular estate asset. Reprehensible beneficiaries cannot secure assets for themselves without the help of lawyers involved in these illegal transactions. For example, my brother, #3, was obligated to repay our late Mother's Trust for the value of the dealership she allowed him to run which was valued at over twenty million dollars. In cutting a Sweetheart Deal with the co-trustee and estate attorneys, #3's responsibility for repayment was drastically reduced, by his attorneys, to only four million dollars thus cheating his siblings out of their rightful share of this valuable family asset. This gave #3, and his wife, a sixteen million dollar financial advantage never intended by our parents. Additionally this secret deal was accomplished with NO APPRAISAL. I'm sure the IRS would have objected to this.

Lawyers know legal maneuvers to delay and drag out a possible estate settlement. Prolonged legal fights are often deliberately designed to ruin one person financially. Few people can afford to keep paying lawyers over long periods of time. Justice is not swift and it doesn't come cheap, if it comes at all.

It is said that you get as much justice in this country as you can afford. Sadly, this is often a reality. Justice and fairness do not always co-exist, and it will cost you tremendously. Negotiation beats litigation when at all possible.

Some lawyers will use emotional distress as a weapon. Opposing attorneys will exploit someone's emotional state to their client's advantage. Few of us have the will fight when our hearts have been devastated by the loss of a parent, let alone our entire family. Lawyers know that. It often makes their job easier.

Many lawyers will exploit fragile family relationships, throw fuel on the fires of family disagreements, and ultimately contribute to the destruction of your family. Ultimately their goal is to make as much money from your family's misery not necessarily to see swift resolutions to estate disputes. The more money in the estate, the more dissension within the family, the better for them.

The most dangerous and destructive attorneys are those who

refuse to follow the Rule of the Law. Many get away with it because the system is so overwhelmed with cases there is no way to police them. Holding their feet to the fire, legally, becomes too time-consuming and costly for most of us, which is what they count on. The attorneys I witnessed lying under oath did so with no threat of reprisal. Their oath meant nothing, and they knew it.

Generally speaking, it is women who outlive men, therefore, it is usually women who end up with the estate. So why does gender discrimination often exist in estate distributions? I believe for the same reason it exists in other facets of society. Many men still believe a woman's financial rights should be limited. It's that simple. And that sad.

49

CHOOSING THE RIGHT ATTORNEY

The first thing to remember when you decide to hire a lawyer to work with you in drawing up your will is that they will be working for you. They may be familiar with legal procedures but chances are they have little knowledge of your family or history. Most people find an attorney through word of mouth. Talk to trusted friends. Even if they have hired lawyers they disliked, at least you will discover whom to avoid. Lawyers, like most professionals, usually police their colleagues. Ethical and honest attorneys will be aware of the bottom feeders, those who show blatant disregard for the Law. Do some research. Ask your tax attorney if he can recommend an estate attorney. Be careful of paid advertisements. They never tell you the true story about an attorney.

Interview prospective candidates. Shop around. Start an outline of your desires for your estate. Prepare your thoughts, list your heirs, additionally, list your assets before your meeting. Outline your situation clearly and include pertinent documents, names and addresses. Trust your instincts. There is no reason to become drinking buddies with your attorney but you do need to find one who will respect your values. In retrospect, the attorneys hired (by others) to represent my Mother never reflected her values or wishes for her estate; therefore it was easy to disregard her will. Take into account their personality, their level of experience, and their ability to communicate wisely. Make sure your attorney takes the time to meet you. Establishing a working relationship with the attorney who will facilitate your estate will bring you tremendous peace of mind for the remainder of your life. It is a good feeling to know you have an updated Will in place should the inevitable happen.

50

FACING THE INEVITABLE

When any estate nightmare occurs there is always a lot of blame to go around. I have to be fair and include my parents' part in contributing, no matter how inadvertent, to the final outcome of their estate. My Mom and Dad were a product of their time. They also never intended to hurt their children whom they loved very much. Still, they made mistakes. My parents were chauvinistic and secretive people. My brothers were always given financial information about my Dad's business. Information denied their daughters because of gender bias. I was loved, but I knew my status was second-class in my family. I was never going to win my Dad's approval by simply being female and I wasn't going to win his respect by being cute and ditzy like my sister. Consequently, I became the responsible daughter, the person who welcomed family obligations even from a very young age.

I became more educated, more accomplished, than all the women (and most of the men) in my family. I had (God-given) talent no one else in the family had. Daddy didn't have to buy me a career. I built my business step by step, by myself. As a result, I grew a backbone my siblings resented. Mom used to ask me, her most sensitive child, how I got to be so strong. My answer was simple. I had no protective husband to rely on in my daily life.

I had no one to fight my battles, to right my wrongs, to slay my dragons. I was not by nature and temperament a fighter. I once had an Italian sister-in-law who loved to argue and fight because it got her juices flowing. Not me. I never fought unless I had to, until someone backed me into a corner. Over time, standing up for myself, when I believed an injustice had occurred, help build my character.

I would come to understand that most people today are not willing to fight, truly lay it all on the line, for what they believe. I don't believe my parents' generation, the "Greatest Generation" fit this description, but it is inherent in my generation, the "Baby Boomer Generation."

Healthy skills for resolving disputes within my family did not exist. Without discussion you could be ostracized, banished, isolated, excluded, and exiled.

Your name was never mentioned. You ceased to exist. The children of "offended" siblings were forbidden to have contact with the accused. The judge and jury convicted you in absentia. In my family, as in many, democracy did not exist. I saw my brothers wrangle for control for years prior to my Dad's death. The jealousy and competition between my siblings and their spouses was stomach-turning. Never was it more evident than during holidays. The antagonist displays for superiority at Christmas were downright hedonistic. I wasn't about to subject myself to the who-can-spend-the-most-and-win-Dad-and-Mom's-approval game. My income couldn't begin to compete with my brothers. I did, however, have one advantage and I thanked God for my creative gifts. I always thought of gifts that no one else imagined and they made lasting impressions. Maybe that's what got me into trouble?

No matter what my six siblings ever did or would one day do to hurt me; I never stopped loving the healthy parts of them. Their rejection was never going to control my love, just as it had not controlled Mom and Dad's love. It took years for me to discover this. When you give from your heart and you are rejected, it says more about the recipient of the gift than it says about you, the giver. No matter what I would ever achieve in life or who I would become, in the eyes of my siblings (clearly demonstrated by their actions) I would never be considered a peer, an equal. I had learned that love was conditional in this club. But how high a price was I willing to pay for admission?

Years after Dad's death, I was home sick one day and saw my brother, #5, on the Oprah Winfrey show. I did not catch the entire program, but I saw her recognize my brother for having donated a car from his (Mom's) dealership to an unfortunate lady. I watched in shock while Oprah and most of America applauded my brother as a good man. I was shocked especially since I knew the truth about his character. I buried my head in my pillow and cried. Mom and I both knew, at that point in time, my baby brother had been stealing from her for years.

Mom died without speaking to two of her sons. Number five was one of them. Personally, I would have welcomed Mom's approval rather than Oprah's.

51

KEEPING GROUNDED

Concentration camp survivor Victor Frankl wrote that "to live is to suffer, to survive is to find meaning in the suffering." I have spent my life seeking to find meaning in the abuse my Mother and I suffered at the hands of my siblings. The final straw was the estate dispute and the injustice that I will have to live with for the rest of my life. You cannot suffer the kind of extreme abuse tethered to a family like mine for more than half a century and not have battle scars so deep that you head for the nearest bunker whenever a car backfires. You learn to live on the edge of apprehension and fear tags you heels. You yearn for and pray for healing but it is often slow to come, if ever.

The emotional and financial abuse of the settlement stays with me no matter how much I try to shove it to the back of my mind. The psychological trauma continues to haunt me often in my dreams. As one of my best friends once said to me, "You cannot put a time limit on injustice." She's right. Once you have suffered something you live with it forever. When someone you love is victimized by the injustice of white-collar crime, the suffering goes deeper than you can imagine.

There is no lower human being than one willing to take advantage of the most vulnerable among us—an elderly parent. Though Mom knew about the sweetheart deals favoring sons who had no intention of repaying their family debts, she had no knowledge about the legal games being played by attorneys she paid and trusted to follow her instructions. Like most of us, she trusted the system. She had no idea the extent of corruption surrounding her estate. Even if she had known, I doubt if she had the remedy to stop it. No one is immune from potential estate problems.

When God gave us the Ten Commandments, He was very specific when He said, "Honor thy Father and thy Mother." He never put a time limit on this rule. God never said, 'Honor your Mother until she's nearly eighty and you want her money.' We were also given commandments not to covet another's goods. He was also pretty emphatic about not having any other gods before him. Worshiping money is the worship of another kind of god. What part of "Thou shall not steal" didn't they get?

*****

Death ends a life, not a relationship. Death did not end my relationship with my parents; it only changed it. I believe Mom and Dad now have full knowledge of earthly matters and know exactly what happened to their estate. I know the level of greed, which ultimately swallowed their fortune, and destroyed their family and legacy, would have horrified them.

Greed elevates the elitist into believing that if they had more worldly possessions they are better than others. More valuable. More important. The question we must ask is: more important than whom? If worldly possessions prove a person's relevance, why were beautiful souls like Pope John Paul II and (Saint) Mother Teresa mourned by millions from all faiths? Why did we honor these penniless people who left no worldly goods behind? They left nothing but a legacy of love for all and respect for the most humble among us. Those were the kinds of people my Mother and Father admired and they gave generously to charities to support that kind of mission.

52

SUSAN'S TRUISMS

While chatting with a dear friend recently, I was asked to include a few of what I refer to as my "truisms," phrases I've collected over the years which ring true in all our lives. Here is a list of my favorites I wanted to share:

Never assume others—even in your immediate family—think the way you do, or share your same values. Sharing DNA is not the same as sharing the same values.

People's lives are always a "pattern of behavior."

Many men will lie under oath. The sacred practice of giving your word before God is often meaningless in today's society.

The word "family" can be redefined to include individuals whose relationships with you are far richer and deeper than those binding by blood ties.

Courage isn't the absence of fear. It is a moving forward despite the fear. You cannot have a healthy life without courage.

Individuals who had no respect for you in life, will exhibit less respect for you after death.

Many people with financial wealth suffer from spiritual and emotional poverty.

Making easy money is more addictive than alcohol.

Never tether your children financially, unless you plan to outlive them.

One of the greatest difficulties is learning to "let go" of the hope of having healthy relationships with loved ones who live limited, addictive lives.

Despite having pain in your heart, you can have joy in your soul.

Never sell your soul, or compromise your values to anyone for any amount of money. You'll never forgive yourself if you do.

Fortunes don't make a man, they expose him.

53

FOR THE RECORD

No parent ever wants to believe their child is capable of being evil or doing evil deeds. I think that's the reason many parents keep giving their children (well into adulthood) chance after chance after chance to get it right—finally. I know that's how my Mom and Dad thought.

In choosing, (or in my family's case) re-choosing their choice of executor(s) they were saying here is one LAST chance for you to get something right, boys.

Wrong!

Irresponsible people don't suddenly become responsible overnight, and no one's pending death will ever change that.

Sorry, if this insults the parent who wants their adult child to be their executor despite their criminal history. I believe it would be a huge mistake.

My parents made that mistake. Additionally, in my opinion, it's a bad idea to tether all your children together financially. My parents' also made that mistake in creating "limited family partnerships" they shackled me together (financially) with my siblings who had long histories of irresponsible spending. How was that going to work to my advantage? Obviously, it didn't.

I know my parents would be heartbroken by how I was treated and the resulting outcome. They never imagined their sons (or hired advisors) capable of such malevolence.

I don't blame them. I understand them. When I looked at Dad, then later Mom, in their coffins—all regrets were forgiven. All I wanted was just one more day to tell them how much I loved them.

What hurt most in the final outcome was being denied the capital to donate land for a park in my parents' name as well as scholarships for deserving students at schools my parents' supported.

When first approached with the concept of a park named for our parents in Dad's home state, my six siblings objected unanimously.

At least I tried, Mom and Dad.

54

UPDATE: HOW CAN THEY DO THAT?

Four years after my families' estate issues ended, or so I thought, I received a letter from a law firm down south informing me I had been named a defendant in a lawsuit. Disheartened, I learned that my brother, #5, had filed bankruptcy two years earlier, walking away from millions of dollars of debt. As a result, his creditors joined forces in suing all his brothers and sisters, living as well as dead, for monies they sought to recover, from whatever source possible.

Since I had not seen my brother in nearly a decade, and had no knowledge of his business dealings, ever, my reaction was, HOW CAN THEY DO THAT?

I came to understand that since I was paid a distribution from our Mother's estate, my brother's creditors claimed that distribution might have been illegal and thus recoverable in their eyes for huge debts incurred by my brother.

As inconceivable as it seemed, the reality was I was forced to hire a law firm in his state to defend me and protect the limited inheritance I was able to secure for myself. I learned that if the creditors prevailed, my obligation could have been as high as $750,000.00 for "my share" of repaying his creditors. A staggering amount, which would have sent me into bankruptcy. I stood to lose everything I had, all over again!

I cooperated with the attorneys I was forced to hire in my brother's state, in every way possible having saved fifteen bankers boxes full of legal documents from my estate dispute with my family. Since I was able to provide original records from my prolonged court battles against my corrupt brothers, I was able to prove to the attorneys for the creditors that I had no knowledge or history of any fraudulent transfers of family funds to this brother or any other member of my family. I never had access to, nor touched, one cent of family money—EVER. My brothers made sure of that. As a direct result, I was "dismissed" from the lawsuit, but not before spending upwards of thirty thousand dollars in legal fees and three months of enormous stress, which compromised my health.

I never learned who sued me, nor did any member of my family ever contact me. I have come to the conclusion that I will never be free of the corruption in my family as long as my siblings live. Their lives are so habitually disruptive; they continue to leave a wake of destruction behind them—sucking in innocent victims. It has become a painful reality of my life, always waiting for the other shoe to drop.

   I have paid an incredible price for membership in this family. My hope is to live the remainder of my life without interference. My journey continues....

55

MOURNING ON MANY LEVELS: HOW I SURVIVED

When I look back, I began the process of mourning long before the deaths of my Mom and Dad. I began mourning the loss of healthy family relationships, which became impossible, as each of my siblings succumbed to addiction.

For whatever reason my siblings made the choice to drink, no one forced them into it. Those choices separated us permanently.

Only one of my brothers (#4) admitted to me he was an alcoholic. The narcissist brother (#3) admitted to my attorney that he and his brothers WERE drunks, "But because they had never been to AA meetings they could NOT be called alcoholics."

I could not believe the sheer stupidity of this remark.

People often ask me how I survived losing my beloved parents, my home, my studio, my ranch, my rightful inheritance, and my entire family. I have only one answer: my Faith.

One of the most beautiful things about my Father was his great spirituality, his great faith in God. From as far back as I can remember, I could feel my Dad's huge hand cradle mine, as we would kneel before the altar in prayer. This was even before I knew what prayer was. I would watch my Daddy when he thought I was not looking from behind my long dark sausage curls. His eyes were closed and at times he was so still it seemed like he was hardly breathing. When Dad was finished praying, he would open his eyes and he would have a beautiful, peaceful smile on his face. Like the face of an angel who looked like my Daddy and smelled of Old Spice aftershave. I wanted that feeling and sought that same spiritual connection all my life.

It was the example set by my Father that drew me toward that spirituality. It has sustained me throughout my life. If I had not been grounded in my Christian faith, I know I could never have survived the heartbreak of watching my family implode. I know this because, until it happened, I had never been subjected to so many evil people for such an extended period of time. Everything I believed in was under attack, and the stress was nearly unbearable.

Thank God I got into therapy. I needed help and I wasn't too proud to ask for it. I was willing to work to discover what went wrong, and to unravel the secrets never before discussed at home.

I had studied addiction for many years in an attempt to understand what was happening to my family. I had witnessed blackout stages with several family members who drank to the point of annihilation. I had suffered the effects of my brothers' extreme narcissism and bigotry toward me because I was a single woman. I had witnessed disturbing sociopathic behavior, which alarmed other individuals close to me. As a victim of abuse, I was outnumbered and outgunned by men intent on taking away everything I had.

When I was younger, I was determined to support my siblings because they were family. However, standing by individuals with a long history of abusive, dishonest behavior did not make my siblings, or their spouses, decent people.

Alcoholics are not comfortable around sober, responsible people so it was not hard for me to figure out why my siblings despised me.

I saw addiction as a progressive, isolating journey that was rooted in selfishness.

My Father use to say, "Susie, selfish people are never happy people. There is never enough money, power, fame, adulation to fill up the void in their hearts." He knew what he was talking about.

A few days after Dad's funeral Mom showed me a file she found in Dad's office containing hundreds of un-cashed checks to my Father from people he had helped over many years. Mom never knew about the checks. Just as Dad wished.

My Father once told me his favorite movie was 'The Magnificent Obsession' which made a lasting impression on me as well. Now I knew why. Not unlike the main character in the story, a successful doctor whose sudden death reveals his "obsession" to help others—secretly—with his financial gifts, my late Father had lived his life the same way. I remember telling Mom, we'll never know how many people he's helped, as in the movie, the recipient is told never to reveal the source of the gift. I got goosebumps to discover this secret philanthropic side of my Father.

Sadly, the only time I remember my Father regretting his generosity was on his deathbed when he told me the biggest mistake of his life was buying the dealerships for his sons. He said to me, "Susie, they forgot where it came from."

People don't lie on their deathbeds. Mom repeated the same quote many times.

It broke both their hearts.

*****

I use to wonder why I became so controversial in my family, and why they took legal (and illegal) steps to rob me of my inheritance. What sins had I committed to warrant my ostracism?

Looking back I don't believe it was anything I did, I think it was who I was.

People always compared me to my Father, the one person my siblings despised most.

Dr. M. Scott Peck reminds us on page 278 of *The Road Less Traveled* that "Evil people hate the light because it reveals themselves to themselves. They hate goodness because it reveals their badness." The gospel according to Saint John reiterates the same message:

John 3:20-21

20 Everyone who does evil hates the light, and will not come into the light for fear that their deeds will be exposed. 21 But whoever lives by the truth comes into the light, so that it may be seen plainly that what they have done has been done in the sight of God.

If my brothers and their attorneys were honest businessmen, why hide their actions from my Mother—their client?

Why all the secrecy? It's simple, people who do evil deeds need the cover of darkness to do their work. It doesn't take much of a man to steal from an old lady. Especially when the old lady is your own Mother. I am reminded by the verse Jesus spoke himself, "Whatever you do to the least of these, you do to Me." (Matt 25:40)

Who qualifies as "The least of these" more than a 79-year-old widow?

In retrospect, I never had a chance of receiving my rightful inheritance. The deck was stacked against me long before Mom was killed in the fire. I was once naïve about wills and trusts and what makes them succeed or fail. I'm not naïve anymore. Aside from the corruption in my own family, it never occurred to me that many attorneys deliberately lie, not only to their own clients, but also under oath. So what is the point of the Rule of Law? What law gives an officer of the court a license to steal?

Every word in this book is the truth. No one could have made up my story. For every event included, there are hundreds more not included.

Tragically my estate nightmare was the result of "the perfect storm" bringing together a dysfunctional family with advisors whose only goal was to exacerbate problems delaying resolutions to ensure their own financial gain.

In the ensuing years since being blackmailed, I have heard countless accounts from people with their own disastrous stories regarding the distribution of their parents possessions. I have seen a grown man tear up, thirty years after his Father's death, recalling what he believed to be an injustice when his stepmother sold his beloved Father's tools at a garage sale deliberately depriving him of a gift his Dad promised would one day be his.

It's NOT always about the money, because all too often, there isn't that much money left at the end of a person's life. What most often breaks our hearts is the sentimental, emotional attachments we have to our parents through the things that mattered most to them.

I wrote my story as a wake-up call to good sons and daughters—unsuspecting victims of the deceitful thieves ready to spring into action when we are at our most vulnerable, the death of our loved ones.

My hope is that my experience will help educate and encourage you to take a more active role in determining the outcome of your own "estate," for the sake of your family and your legacy. It's the most unselfish thing you can do for those you love most.

56

"FOR WHOM THE BELL TOLLS"

To say that I suffered more than my share of indignities at the hands of my brothers only tells part of my story. The cold-blooded way their wives contributed to my family's complete downfall, and my suffering specifically, tells the story of women so heartless and cruel they demonstrated they were (and still are) incapable of common human decency.

When my Mother was killed, not one of my brothers' wives was kind enough to call and let me know. Not one expressed one word of condolence to me—ever.

Two years later when my brother (#2) died, not one person from my family called to tell me. The "estranged" sister-in-law who wrote his obituary deliberately omitted my name as a sister.

History repeated itself when a few years later the wife of one of my former employees called, out of the blue, to offer her sympathies on the deaths of TWO of my brothers, (#1 and #4) who died three days apart in two different countries. When I asked, "Which brothers?" she was horrified that, again, no one in my family had enough respect to inform me of their deaths. By the time I found out, both had already been buried.

For the second and third times, my name was deliberately excluded from their obituaries.

A few years later I was "copied" a court document on a case-long defunct—which referenced the death of my sister. For the FIFTH time, not one person in my family had the respect I deserved to inform me my only sister was gone. Internet searches revealed nothing of her death. Not the date, or cause, or place—nothing.

By now my family had refined the art of concealment so totally not even seasoned investigators have been able to discover any details surrounding my sister's death.

Incredibly, only a few weeks ago I got a call from a cousin who discovered my youngest brother (#5) had died last year.

Again, no one told me. All we could find on the Internet were two sentences naming his two children and nothing else. He was ten years younger than me. It never occurred to me I would outlive him.

Despite our differences and estrangement we were once family and I cried over each loss. I mourned the children we once were in happier times—before the money, before the "in-laws", and before the addiction to alcohol.

Whatever egregious offenses I was accused of committing towards my family, no evidence has ever revealed any attempt on my part to deliberately harm them in any way. I never had the desire or inclination to do so. What motive would I have? I had no power, no time, no desire and no money to take on the "mafia".

For a girl who devoted her formative years to her family, who dreamed of being a wife and mother all her life, but never saw that dream become a reality, what possible motivation would I have to damage the family I DID have?

It makes no sense.

Don't you think I paid a high enough price, suffered enough pain, and endured enough indignities to last a lifetime?

I've nearly run out of family to torture me. Only one brother remains, (the narcissist). All the other seven members of my core family are now gone.

Maybe, for once, I'll get lucky and outlive the bastard.

57

"AGGRAVATION FOLLOWS ME"

My Mother always joked about wanting to write a book about her fifty years of married life with all the good, the bad, and the ugly stories called, *Aggravation Follows Me*.

She never accomplished this goal, but in many ways, this book is as much Mom's story as it is mine.

The older I get the more I realize how disrespected my Mother was for two particular reasons: her age and her gender. I cannot think of even one man mentioned in this entire book (aside from my Dad) who treated her with honesty and respect. Not one.

My Mother lived her final years in fear of her sons and their hired attorneys, whom she knew were stealing from her.

She was a warm and generous lady who deserved better, much better.

No one will ever convince me that the total failure to distribute my Mother's estate was a result other than gender discrimination and extreme elder abuse.

Since women generally outlive men (statistically 73.4 years for men, to 80.1 years for women) I wonder how many women have been cheated out of their own inheritance as well as their right to determine their heirs?

I wonder—

Are elderly rich widows deliberately targeted by the legal profession as "unworthy" recipients of their husband's trusts? Irrefutably my Mother's five sons certainly believed so.

Mom's protestations fell on deaf ears over and over and over again.

How was this not elder abuse?

As the years have passed, despite working hard to move beyond my estate nightmare, I am still most angry about the abuse suffered by my Mother. It was deliberate, it was calculated, it was criminal and it was totally unnecessary. As for me, I cannot forgive the sister-in-law who stole my Mother's jewelry, recipes, and personal effects.

She violated the sacred bond between my Mother and I. She felt entitled when she had no right to interfere in the final arrangements between a Mother and her daughter.

Sorry, but there are offenses I find unforgivable. I know my Mom would agree.

*****

Remember that little girl who showed up at that birthday party in dungarees? She's still wearing jeans, and you know what? It suits her better than a party dress.

58

THE GREATEST GIFT OF ALL

The last time I saw my Mother alive was January 20, 2000. We had enjoyed a wonderful visit and I was leaving for the airport to catch a flight home.

As we hugged goodbye, we both started crying. I told Mom how much I loved her and that I always tried to be a good daughter. At that point she looked me straight in the eyes and said,

"Susan, you were the perfect daughter, you were way too good for this family, and I cannot say that about any of my other children."

Thanks, Mom, for validating my entire life. They can't take that away from me.

ACKNOWLEDGMENTS

One of the sad realities in writing this true story is my inability to credit those individuals, by their real names, for their incredible contributions to this book as well as my life. They know how much I appreciate and love them for their unflinching support.

BIBLIOGRAPHY

Bernstein, Albert J., *Emotional Vampires*

Bove, Jr. Esq., Alexander A. *Wills, Estates, Trusts*

Crier, Catherine, *The Case Against Lawyers*

Donne, John, *For Whom the Bell Tolls* English (1572–1631)

Feinman, Jay M., *1001 Legal Words You Need To Know*

Frankl, Victor, *Man's Search for Meaning*

Nakken, Craig, *The Addicted Personality*

Peck, Dr. M. Scott, *People of the Lie*; *The Road Less Traveled*

Prager, Dennis, *Happiness Is a Serious Problem*

Thurmann, Dr. Chris, *The Lies We Believe*

Williams, Roy and Preisser, Vic, *Preparing Heirs*

Willis, Thayer Cheatham, *Navigating the Dark Side of Wealth*

ANYWAY

The following poem hung in the Calcutta office of Mother Teresa. Its message inspires and comforts me every day of my life.

ANYWAY

People are unreasonable, illogical, and self-centered,

LOVE THEM ANYWAY

If you do good, people will accuse you of selfish, ulterior motives,

DO GOOD ANYWAY

If you are successful, you win false friends and true enemies,

SUCCEED ANYWAY

The good you do will be forgotten tomorrow,

DO GOOD ANYWAY

Honesty and frankness make you vulnerable,

BE HONEST AND FRANK ANYWAY

What you spent years building may be destroyed overnight,

BUILD ANYWAY

People really need help but may attack if you help them,

HELP ANYWAY

Give the world the best you have and you'll get kicked in the teeth,

GIVE THE WORLD THE BEST YOU'VE GOT—ANYWAY.

The Pieta
Painting by Susan Sparrow

www.ingramcontent.com/pod-product-compliance
Lightning Source LLC
Chambersburg PA
CBHW050320120526
44592CB00014B/1990